ROYAL YACHTING ASSOCIATION
RACE TRAINING MANUAL

Royal Yachting Association Race Training Manual

Jim Saltonstall
RYA National Racing Coach

Published in association with the Royal Yachting Association

HEINEMANN:LONDON

William Heinemann Ltd
10 Upper Grosvenor Street, London W1X 9PA
LONDON   MELBOURNE   TORONTO
JOHANNESBURG   AUCKLAND

First published 1983
© J.E.R. Saltonstall and the Royal Yachting Association 1983

434 67170 3

Frontispiece: Practice makes perfect!

Filmset by CK Typesetters Ltd., Sutton, Surrey
Printed and bound in Spain by
Mateu Cromo Artes Graficas, S.A.

Contents

Foreword

All of us are good at doing something either at work or at play, but we could go through life without ever having the opportunity to pass on that skill to others. It is the prime function of the sports coach to seek out and encourage others with sporting skills who will likewise be able to pass on those special skills to equally keen sportsmen who wish to better their sporting performance.

It was whilst I was putting together the National Race Training Scheme that I had the good fortune to involve Navy Coach, Jim Saltonstall, and I persuaded him to run the pilot courses for the Queen Mary Sailing Club. Out of these courses came an enthusiasm and dedication which eventually landed him the full-time appointment of RYA National Racing Coach.

In four years, he has refined and expanded the scheme to include the National Youth and Women's Squads and schemes for adult club members.

His individual and somewhat unorthodox coaching style and his fierce loyalty to his homeland—Yorkshire!—appeals to all those who fall under his care.

As with all coaching manuals, this book is intended as a guide to individuals and trainers alike, enabling readers to formulate their own paths to perfection, but as with all worthwhile goals it will entail a considerable amount of hard labour, often a 'life sentence'.

One of the most important aspects of the book is the sense of achievement and pleasure it generates. Sailing should be enjoyed, otherwise there is little point in embarking on such a complex and often perplexing study of the inter-relationship of wind, water, weather, equipment and tactics. One of the greatest bars to the enjoyment of training sessions is a coach who blindly follows a book such as this as being 'the official RYA method'. The reason that the author is such an outstanding coach is that he is prepared to try new techniques and abandon exercises which do not fit the coaching situation he is faced with. I am sure that this manual will become a standard work in the hands of skilled, open-minded sailors.

Competition sailing is extremely demanding and can only be totally rewarding if you match your ambition to your capabilities. You will only know your own capabilities by matching your skills against others of known ability.

Bob Bond

RYA Training Manager

Acknowledgments

I would sincerely like to thank the following people, whose help and support over the years have enabled me to write this book.

First, my father Peter, John and Les Rix, Bob Blythe OBE, and the Royal Yorkshire Yacht Club for my initial apprenticeship in the sport. Without their knowledge and expertise I would never have made it!

Secondly, the Royal Navy for allowing me to develop in the sport both as a helmsman and a coach, and I would particularly like to thank Captain Norman Fitzgerald for his support in Royal Navy dinghy racing.

Thirdly, to Hugh Bailey who has done a marvellous job at all our race training seminars helping to produce slides for race training purposes, and to whom I am indebted for the majority of the photographs in this book.

To both Bob and Maggie Bond for giving me this opportunity to express my race training thoughts and for helping me over the past four years.

Finally, to my wife Christine and son Jeremy, for allowing me the time to do the job which I thoroughly enjoy.

Jim Saltonstall
RYA National Racing Coach

Introduction

Messing about in boats conjures up lazy, idyllic days spent gently sailing in rivers, lakes or sheltered coastal waters. Cruising also has a magic of its own, whether coastal hopping or sailing into the sunset in search of faraway places like Cherbourg or maybe the Greek Islands........

Racing—that's different!

The sport of dinghy and yacht racing has become very complex and competitive in recent years and most certainly will become more so in the future. This interest and competition has led to much progress and development in the shape and construction of hulls, sails and all the rigging, fittings and 'goodies' that make up a modern racing dinghy or yacht.

Racing is a complex activity, a battle against the elements, a contest between one sailor and another, one boat and another. Some say it is a game of chance. If so, it is a game played to a set of very strict rules and one which places great and varied demands on the participants if they are to have any chance at all.

A present-day contestant is required to know the rules of the game intimately, to have many skills each dependent on another, and in modern dinghies in particular, racing requires an athletic prowess and special physique which was never demanded of past champions.

This has resulted in the necessity for race training. Because of the importance other countries are placing on their race training, it has become imperative for Britain to give much more serious consideration and attention to its race training programme involving both youth and adults.

Since 1977, the RYA has been aiming to raise our standards of racing at all levels—Club, Regional, National and International. Club racing is important in order to ensure that high standards start at this level and filter through to the more advanced stages of racing. The RYA places a strong emphasis on structured racing courses for youth so as to train our future champions at an early age and ensure a high degree of proficiency.

To a large extent, three factors determine whether the racing participant will be a Club, Regional, National or International racing sailor. These are ambition, finance and time. Ambition decides the amount of effort that has to be put into the sport, and those thinking of taking up racing must consider their financial means, as well as the time they have available to devote to the training and preparation involved in racing. These three factors apart, it is then up to the individual to practise—as in any sport, practice is the only way to achieve improvement.

This manual is divided into two parts. The aim of Part 1 is to improve your racing; concentrating on preparation, boat handling, tuning, starting, tactics, compass work, mark rounding, crewing and Racing Rules 31-46. It explains the right and wrong way to go about various sailing manoeuvres giving those extra seconds necessary to gain the advantage. Part 2 explains the structure of the RYA, the courses available, advice on teaching methods and the RYA Race Training Exercises.

Whatever the aim of the racing sailor, whether it be to win the Club Championship or a World Championship, the maximum effort should always be put into preparation and training; but above all, racing is to be enjoyed. After all, it is the best sport in the world!

PART 1
How to Improve your Racing

1
Preparation

Preparation before a race is a very important part of racing, and can be divided into the following four categories:

- self preparation;
- boat preparation;
- geographical and tidal preparation;
- last minute preparation.

These will be considered below.

Self Preparation

PHYSICAL FITNESS

One of the best ways to get fit and remain fit is to spend all your spare time sailing!

There are three main ways to keep fit:

1. An exercise programme.
2. A second stamina and strength sport.
3. Sail as much as possible.

In addition to being generally fit, you must do specific training for your particular job in the boat as a helm or a crew. There are six basic types of boat and these are as follows:

- singlehander
- doublehander
- trapezing
- non-trapezing
- small keel boats
- large keel boats

The fitness training programme, for example, for a Finn or Laser sailor would be different from that of a Flying Dutchman helmsman or that of a trapeze crew, and again, different to the fitness training of a Merlin Rocket crew. Another point to consider is whether you require long-term endurance and stamina as in big boat offshore racing, or short bursts of sustained energy as required in high performance dinghies at World and Olympic level. Likewise, the fitness required to win a race at club level is nowhere near that required at World Championship level—depending on the standard of racing at the club! All of these points must be considered carefully before starting to train.

The length of time you should train before an event is also important. Training should start at least three months before, not three days or three hours! By this time it is much too late and quite pointless.

The following exercises suggest an outline which should be used on a daily basis during a physical fitness training programme.

Appendix II should also be referred to as it provides a physical fitness training performance chart which gives an idea of the level of fitness that should be achieved within certain time limits by both men and women.

1. *Jogging*

It is a good idea to get into the practice of jogging every day for approximately thirty minutes for endurance, stamina and general warm-up. This should then be followed by a series of exercises designed to improve leg, stomach and arm muscles as follows:

(a) Leg muscles

- hopping on the spot, one/both legs;
- knees and legs slowly bending and stretching;
- stride jumps;
- star jumps;
- tuck jumps (knees to chest).

(b) Stomach muscles

- sit-ups;
- V-sits;
- wall bar hanging–legs raised to right angles.

(c) Arm muscles

- press-ups;
- squat thrusts;
- arms out straight in front, rolling a weight up and down;
- pull-ups (chinning the bar).

2. *Weight training*

This may be done by singlehanders, e.g. Finn, Laser and Contender sailors and also by trapeze crews and big boat crews. Weight training falls into two categories:

(a) heavy weights—slow repetition
(b) light weights—quick repetition

Weight training builds up muscle weight and therefore all-up body-weight. It is important never to weight train alone; it must be done under supervision.

3. *Swimming*

As an alternative sport to keep-fit, swimming will give you all-round fitness and stamina.

Whatever job you do when racing, remember that flexibility in the body muscles plays a major role both in light winds when it is important to move nimbly around the boat, and in strong winds when endurance and stamina are needed. Stay away from physical contact sports. You do not want to break any bones just before a major event.

There are many good books on physical training exercises and these should be referred to.

Only the fittest, mentally and physically, will win!

Boat Preparation

Once you have decided on the type of boat you wish to race and have acquired it, the next step is to prepare the boat for racing. The preparation can be broken down into four main areas as follows:

- internal layout—fittings and sheets
- outer hull finish
- boards and blades
- measurement.

The complexity of the boat will dictate how many hours work it will take each week to put your boat in racing trim and having reached this standard, keep it in trim. For example, it will take an average of 14–16 hours per week to keep a Flying Dutchman fully operational, whereas an Optimist would only take 1–4 hours per week.

INTERNAL LAYOUT

Keep the layout of the boat as simple as possible, remove all unnecessary gadgets. This will help to reduce three important factors:

1. The all-up overall weight of the boat.
2. The risk of gear failure.
3. The all-up expense of the boat.

Fit into the boat only the essential fittings, making sure that they are securely fixed and operational. Where running rigging is concerned, make the system as friction-free as possible.

Always check standing and running rigging, fittings and sheaves prior to each race. If you neglect this regular check, one day you will inevitably have to retire from an important race due to gear failure.

Main, jib and spinnaker sheets should be the minimum thickness required for the job, and such that you can handle them without their cutting into your hands. They should all be calibrated for the correct setting in the various conditions (this is covered in the boat tuning section). Finally, the sheets should be tapered so as to reduce friction and weight throughout the system.

OUTER HULL FINISH

Much work needs to be done on the outer hull of the boat from stem to stern and gunwale to gunwale, to reduce the surface friction and drag. One way of doing this with fibre-glass hulls is initially to rub the whole bottom down with a fine abrasive polish so as to remove all grease and dirt. Follow this with a 600-grade wet and dry sandpaper and finally clean it down again with a fine abrasive polish. Subsequent cleaning sessions can be done using the fine abrasive cleaner—only use the wet and dry sandpaper as required to remove scratches. In the case of a wooden hull, the same principles apply, finishing off with a dull matt finish.

BOARDS AND BLADES

1. *Centreboards and daggerboards*

Within the Class Rules, a boat which is ideally underweight when new, should be brought up to weight with a maximum weight centreboard or daggerboard, which has stiffness athwartships and is fibre-glass coated. In its box, a board should have no play athwartships, but must have the least amount of friction when being raised and lowered. It has been proved in some high performance dinghy classes that to have a gybing centreboard improves pointing ability. This is when the leading edge of the board is allowed to angle slightly to windward.

By raising and lowering the centreboard you are altering the centre of lateral resistance (C of LR) either forward with the board fully down, or progressively aft as you raise the board. In this way, you can control boat balance, weather helm and leeway.

It is important to realise how much board is showing under the boat for the various points of sailing as well as the various wind strengths. To this end you should put your boat on its side and mark on the board the positions required for the various points of sailing as well as the various wind strengths. Mark them with either a felt tipped pen or a calibration strip along the trailing edge.

The finish of the board should be as that of the outer hull, and treated in the same way with a fine abrasive polish or cleaner and 600-grade wet and dry sandpaper.

2. *Rudder blades*

The same criteria apply to rudder blades as to centreboards and daggerboards as far as stiffness and finish are concerned, but with regard to weight, though the rudder blade should be as light as possible, it should not be so light that it snaps whilst 'three sail reaching' in strong winds. The leading edge of the blade should also be relatively thick so that stalling is not experienced when bearing away in the stronger winds when on a reach.

MEASUREMENT

Always make sure that your boat is 'in class'. There is nothing more irritating than to find that the sails do not measure or your sail numbers are in the wrong place, or some other error, after you arrive at a major event. All these things must be checked and dealt with at home.

Geographical and Tidal Preparation

In modern-day racing, success at an important event is two-thirds preparation, and geographical and tidal/current considerations are an essential part of this preparation.

Once you know the date and venue of your next major event, you can begin to make preparations. Start by acquiring a chart and tidal atlas, plus any other useful information, about the area. There may be, if you are lucky, a military meteorological centre nearby willing to give you a weather forecast on a daily basis.

On your chart, plot the racing area (you can do this on a piece of tracing paper—drawn to scale). Theoretically making up your mind as to what you think the wind will do, superimpose the wind pattern over the racing area, taking into consideration the surrounding geographical features.

Once you have worked out the theoretical wind situation (do not forget to work out the sea breezes too), look at the current or tidal situation, observing through your tracing paper whether or not the race area straddles any metre line or sandbanks, with the wind coming from all the main cardinal points.

You can now look at your tidal data and see how it is going to affect you throughout the racing period on a daily basis—whether it is a neap or spring tide. The change of direction of the tide over the racing area, the time and strength, should be sorted out prior to going to the championship.

Try to arrive at the racing venue two or three days prior to the event. Having done all the preparation beforehand you will quickly be able to orientate yourself and put your theories into practice.

This is an important part of pre-race preparation and it is worth doing thoroughly. Psychologically it will give you more confidence as you go into the event.

Last-minute Preparation

Before going to race, carry out the following checks:

CHECKS ASHORE BEFORE GOING AFLOAT

1. *Sailing instructions*
Go through them thoroughly, sort out any queries and take them afloat with you.

2. *Weather forecast*
No wise sailor ever goes to sea without one. This will help you to make a number of important decisions, as follows:

- which sails to use;
- what clothing to wear;
- which way to go up the beat each time;
- to be on the look out for windshifts and cloud formation.

3. *Tidal information*
Races can be won or lost on tidal knowledge alone. You may have the fastest boat, your boat handling might be the best in the fleet, but if you do not know what the tide or current is doing throughout the racing period and all over the racing area, you will not do well and you certainly will not win.

Also remember the stronger the wind, the less important the tide and vice versa, except if you have a strong tide and/or current which varies over the course. All this must be sorted out well beforehand.

4. *Special notices*
Look to see if there are any special notices or rules in force—check the notice-board and look out for the flag *Lima* at the regatta office. This indicates there has been a change in the sailing instructions.

5. *Boat check*
Check your boat before going afloat. Spinnaker poles and safety tallies are the two favourites to be left ashore!

CHECKS AFLOAT BEFORE STARTING

At any major event it will generally pay you to be out on the race area in good time, the only exception being on a reservoir or lake when the start line is only a few minutes away.

Once in the race area spend time checking the following:

1. *Check the wind as often as possible*
You must try to establish what the wind is doing. Is it slowly backing and veering in accordance with the forecast or is it oscillating around a mean direction? Is there a wind bend over the area? All these factors must be checked out during this period. If you do not do this you have tactically lost before you start!

2. *Use this information and your tidal and current data to plan your start*
Once you have this information it will help you to plan your race strategy more confidently and help you decide which way you will go up the all-important first beat.

3. *Keep warm*
During the winter months sail around and keep warm. Sitting around with your sails flogging does both you and the sails no good at all.

4. *Final checks*
Do your final checks in the boat and make sure all is ready in the boat for the start. The final tuning of the boat is also done in this period whilst checking the wind in the racing area.

2
Boat Handling

Good boat handling plays a major role in successful yacht and dinghy racing, and again, practice makes perfect. The younger you start and the more you practise, the more experienced you will be when it comes to top-level competition.

Plate 1. In light winds to windward, balance the boat slightly to leeward.

Each type of dinghy has its own handling characteristics and the only way to discover them is to spend time on the water.

When you change from one class of boat to another, do not try to apply all the same handling techniques to your new class of boat; it will not work. For example, the handling characteristics of a 505 are different from those of a 470.

There are a number of points which are general to boat handling and do not refer to any particular class of boat. These are listed below, followed by a more detailed explanation of each point:

- boat balance: athwartships movement of the boat
- boat trim: fore and aft movement of the boat
- tacking: flat water, waves and roll tacking
- gybing: roll and waves
- beating: flat and choppy water
- holding your position: starting area
- body movement: in relation to waves.

Boat Balance

1. *To Windward*
(a) Light winds:(Plate 1)
   In these conditions the boat must be

balanced to leeward. The amount depends on the shape of the boat underwater. For example, you would not balance a Merlin Rocket to leeward as much as a 420, as you would be increasing the wetted area and surface drag instead of decreasing it.

By balancing the boat to leeward in these conditions you are getting the sails to take their more natural shape with the least amount of wind.

You are now presenting more readily the lee-bow of the boat to the water, making the boat want to point more as she sails to windward and give more feel on the tiller. This slight feel of weather helm is not detrimental to speed unless it is excessive.

Immersing the leeward side of the boat is much more effective in International 14s and National 12s than in a Fireball or a Topper, because of their underwater shape, forward of the mast.

(b) Medium-strong winds:(Plate 2)

In the medium wind range you must work hard at generally keeping the boat as upright as possible to gain maximum power out of the boat. I say generally because with certain types of boat it pays to balance them slightly to windward and with others slightly to leeward. Again this depends on the underwater shape of the boat, in the area either side and forward of the mast; it also depends on the sea state, flat or choppy water; and it depends on the characteristics of the type of boat you sail.

(c) Gusty conditions:

In these conditons it will most certainly pay to sail the boat balanced slightly to windward prior to the gust actually

Plate 2. In medium to strong winds, keep the boat as flat as possible for maximum power.

hitting you, so that when it does hit you, the boat is brought back upright and this is transferred into power driving the boat forward as opposed to heeling the boat to leeward, sliding sideways and broaching. This induces weather helm by use of the tiller, and slows the boat down.

Other times to balance the boat to windward are when trying to put the opposition in a lee-bow situation and also when going into a roll tack or gybe.

2. *Reaching*

(a) Light winds:(Plate 3 *see page 10*)

On a close beam reach, balance the boat

to leeward but if there is enough wind to keep the sails full, balance the boat to windward. In the case of spinnaker boats, have the spinnaker down in the very light winds and concentrate purely on trimming foresail and main. Again by balancing the boat to leeward in these conditions you are reducing the wetted area and surface drag, and getting the sails to take their shape with the least amount of wind. The amount of balance depends on the type of boat, as already mentioned. On a very broad reach it may pay to balance the boat to windward as long as there is enough wind to stop the mainsail from collapsing. If this happens the boat must be balanced to leeward.

(b) Medium-strong winds:(Plate 4 *see page 12*)
In these conditions it pays to keep the boat as flat as possible to get maximum power out of the rig (Fig. 1). If the boat is allowed to balance either way you will be losing power out of the rig and start to broach to leeward or capsize to windward. In the stronger gusty conditions, it will pay with most types of boat to balance the boat slightly to windward.

3. *Running*

(a) Light winds:(Plate 5 *see page 12*)
As long as there is enough wind to prevent the mainsail inverting it will always pay to balance your boat to windward (opposite side to the boom on a dead run) so as to achieve the following:

Plate 3 *opposite*. When reaching in light winds, balance the boat to leeward to help the sails fill and reduce the wetted area and surface drag.

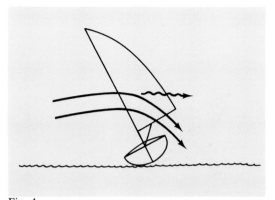

Fig. 1.
(a) Boat balance to windward. Loss of maximum power.

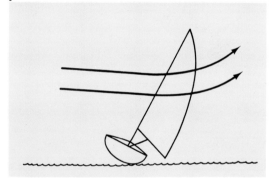

(b) Boat balance to leeward. Loss of maximum power.

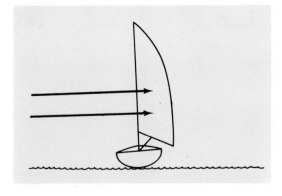

(c) Keep the boat in balance for maximum drive.

Plate 4 *above*. Concentrate on maximum power, keeping the boat flat, when reaching in the medium wind range.

Plate 5 (a) (b) and (c) *below and above right*. Examples of good boat balance to windward in light winds on a dead run.

Plate 6. When running in medium to strong winds, the crew helps to balance and stabilize the boat by sitting on the opposite side of the boat to the helmsman.

- reduce the wetted area and surface drag;
- take the centre of effort (C of E) of the rig more directly above the centre of lateral resistance (C of LR) of the hull;
- raise the outboard end of the boom higher off the water to present more mainsail area higher up to catch what wind there is;
- with spinnaker boats, the spinnaker will now want to appear from behind the mainsail and again catch what wind there is; whereas if the boat was kept upright or worse still, allowed to balance to leeward, the spinnaker would disappear behind the mainsail and achieve nothing!

Plate 7 *right*. Trim the boat down by the bow when sailing to windward in light winds and on flat water.

(b) Medium-strong winds:(Plate 6)

You must work at keeping the boat flat all the time, otherwise you may initiate the 'death roll'! Keeping the boat flat on a dead run in strong winds depends on: trim, kicking strap tension, board position, spinnaker sheet leads and speed—all these points will be discussed under the appropriate headings further on in the manual.

Boat Trim

1. *To Windward*
(a) Light winds:(Plate 7)

In these conditions you must trim the boat down by the bow to achieve the following:

- present more lee-bow to the water so as to increase more feel to the boat and better pointing ability. Again, the amount depends on the shape of the boat forward of the mast, and there is a huge difference between a Topper and a Fireball, National 12s and International 14s as examples.
- to raise the aft flatter sections off the water and reduce the surface drag.
- to place body-weight in the area of the boat which is most buoyant, i.e. either side of the mast.

Plate 8. Good boat trim is essential in medium winds to windward, so as not to upset the pitch of the boat through the waves.

(b) Medium winds:(Plate 8)

In these conditions it is important to work at keeping the maximum waterline length in contact with the water so as not to affect the pitching of the boat over the waves. What you cannot have is the boat trimmed too much by the bow so that you are slamming into waves, or vice versa, where the stern is dragging and the bow being blown off to leeward at the crest of a wave.

(c) Strong winds:(Plate 9)

These winds are normally associated with choppy seas. In these conditions it is important to trim the boat a little further aft when sailing almost head on into the chop on one tack. This results in the boat's pitching over the waves more easily. When sailing parallel to the waves on the other tack, you must trim the boat down by the bow again. You must also assist this movement by upper body torque moving aft as the boat lifts, and forwards as she goes over and down the back of the wave.

Plate 9 (a) *above*. In strong winds to windward, trim the boat slightly further aft to enable the bow to lift more smoothly over the waves.

Plate 9 (b) *left*. Do not overdo it!

2. *Reaching*

(a) Light winds:

The boat must be trimmed down by the bow to reduce the wetted area of the hull in contact with the water.

(b) Medium winds:

Trim the boat so as to keep the waterline in contact with the water over its whole length.

(c) Strong winds:(Plate 10 *see page 16*)

Keep the weight aft. The more powerful the spinnaker and headsail, the more important this is so as to raise the lee-bow off the water. This is critical, especially if hit by a gust, so that you can bear away with the least amount of rudder

Plate 10. A well trimmed boat keeps the lee-bow off the water which enables you to bear away in a gust.

Plate 11. On a running leg in light winds, trim the boat down by the bow so as to reduce surface drag.

movement (thereby reducing the risk of snapping it off!) and it also reduces the risk of stalling, broaching and capsizing to leeward. With the lee-bow off the water, you can bear away without any problem as long as the board is not too far down.

3. *Running*

(a) Light winds:(Plate 11)

Trim the boat down by the bow slightly, again for reasons already mentioned. You may also raise the board all the way, but take care not to over-balance to windward and capsize! You will be relatively all right on flat water, the danger is more likely to occur on the open sloppy sea.

(b) Medium winds:

Maximum waterline length and the boat must be kept flat, as already mentioned.

(c) Strong winds:(Plate 12)

You must trim the boat relatively well aft in these conditions so as to lift the bow off the water and reduce the risk of the 'death roll' movement. This is especially important with boats with sharp, deep, 'V'-shaped sections forward of the mast, because if the bow makes contact with the water it becomes another rudder. The

Plate 12. On a dead run, in a strong breeze, the bow is kept off the water to assist in establishing the balance of the boat.

bow, travelling at speed, wants to flick either left or right depending on which side is in contact, and once this motion starts and the board is either too far up or down, you will either broach to leeward or corkscrew in to windward. Make sure you trim the boat well aft in these conditions to keep the bow up, and present the after flatter sections to the water so that the boat becomes more stable.

Tacking

There is much to be gained or lost by a crew who can or cannot tack a boat properly. We have proved in training that (depending on its length) a boat, correctly tacked on flat water, can gain approximately three to five yards over a boat that is not properly tacked—and on the open sea these distances are increased.

1. *Flat water*

On flat water you can tack a boat without having to consider waves, and it is important to learn to roll tack the boat properly. Plates 13 (a)-(k), 14, 15 and 16 *(on the following pages)* demonstrate the right and wrong way to roll tack, and will now be considered carefully. In Plates 13 (a) and (b), the boat has been allowed to balance to leeward whilst going into the tack. This is wrong, as in order to roll tack correctly, the boat must be spun around the C of LR (as around a five-pence piece rather than sliding around the edge of a pound note). Also in Plates 13 (a)-(e), it is clear that too much rudder has been used to luff and tack the boat which has created a large stern wake. Plates 13 (d)-(k) show good jib work by the crew, allowing the jib to back slightly to speed up the tack before pulling the jib in quickly on the new tack as shown in Plate 13 (i). Good

Plate 13 (a)

Plate 13 (b) *above.*

Plate 13 (c) *above.* Plate 13 (d) *below.*   Plate 13 (e) *above.* Plate 13 (f) *below.*

Plate 13 (g) *above.* Plate 13 (h) *below.*　　　Plate 13 (i) *above.* Plate 13 (j) *below.*

Plate 13 (k) *below.*

teamwork in the boat is shown in Plates 13 (f)-(k) as both the helm and crew cross the boat together to bring the boat upright out of the tack, pulling in the armful of mainsheet, which is eased as the helm crosses the boat. In Plates 14 (a)-(c), the crew is correctly tacking the boat facing aft. In Plates 15 (a)-(c), the boat is being tacked incorrectly

Plate 14 (a)

Plate 14 (b)

Plate 14 (c)

Plate 15 (a)

for the following reasons: 15 (a) the boat is balanced to leeward, with too much tiller movement to leeward, and the helm and crew are not leaning out enough; 15 (b) there is still too much tiller movement to leeward and the helm and crew are crossing the boat too soon; 15 (c) the crew is slow in pulling the jib in on the new tack. Plate 16 *(see page 24)*, shows how to go into a roll tack correctly and the helm and crew are balancing the boat to windward.

2. *Open sea*

On the open sea you are not free to manoeuvre, as you must watch the waves. As a wave lifts the bow, the tiller must be allowed to go to leeward. As the boat comes into the eye of the wind with body-weight to windward, the same wave is passing under

Plate 15 (b)

Plate 15 (c)

Plate 16 *above*

Plate 17 (a) *opposite*. When roll gybing in light winds, cross the boat and correct the balance so that the outboard end of the boom does not hit the water.

Plate 17 (b) *above*. The boom has hit the water, but the helmsman is in a position to prevent the broach and capsize.

Plate 17 (c). What not to do! Too slow in crossing the boat to correct the balance and too much centreboard down. The boom hits the water and the inevitable broach and capsize follow.

the centreboard area. The boat goes through the eye of the wind, body-weight moves across the boat which is now brought upright as the same wave is supporting the new leeward quarter area of the boat, and the boat accelerates off the back of the wave like a surfboard. This sequence depends very much on the length of the boat and the distance between the crests of the waves. In the case of the Flying Dutchman and short distances between crests, we must look for the bigger waves to achieve the same momentum.

Gybing

1. *Light winds—flat water* (Plate 17 *see this and previous pages*)
Roll gybing is important here. This entails rolling the boat to windward first and then bringing the boom over. As it comes over and body-weight is moved across the boat, the boat is brought upright. This prevents the boom hitting the water while maintaining the boat speed out of the gybe.

2. *Strong winds—rough water* (Plate 18)
How many people can honestly say that they have arrived at the gybe mark in this situation without saying 'I wish I was not here'!? Not many, I am sure. So what must be considered to stand a chance of survival?....

(a) Speed. The faster you are going into the gybe, the safer you are, as the wind pressure in the sail is at its weakest.
(b) Do not execute the gybe as you are about to run into the back of a wave in front of you, as this will stop the boat dead, the rig will go forward and you will definitely capsize!
(c) Make sure you trim the boat correctly. You must be well aft so as to raise the bow off the water as much as possible. This releases the enormous pressure switching from one bow to the other as you gybe which if in contact with the water will trip you in.
(d) Board position. Like the bow, if too much board is presented, the pressure switches from one side of the board to the other and you trip over the board. Vice versa, if the board is too far up and you gybe, you will capsize to windward on completion of the gybe! So how much

Plate 18. Gybing in a fresh breeze needs to be executed with speed and confidence. Watch your speed, board position, boat trim and the waves.

board should be down? Well, if you think about it, there is only one answer to that question—enough to stand on once you have capsized! You should have about six to nine inches showing, just enough to act as a skeg to stop the boat from slipping from under you sideways on completion of the gybe.

If you get these four things together, you will stand a chance of survival—get any one of these wrong and you will inevitably capsize.

Beating

The techniques of racing a boat to windward on flat water and on the open sea are completely different and this can be seen when an inland sailor (a puddle sailor) meets a hardened sea sailor. If the race is on flat water, on lakes or reservoirs, the puddle sailor would normally win, and vice versa on the open sea.

1. *Puddle racing*
What do the puddle sailors do, what do they look for, aim for?

(a) The aim is to gain maximum speed and pointing ability. To achieve this they set relatively flat sail/s and also have hard leaches so as to combine speed and pointing ability.

(b) They spend 90% of their time looking at their leading 'tell-tales' watching for a heading wind. When it comes, they tack straight away being freed up on the new tack all the time. It is maybe relevant at this stage to say that you will get frequent wind shifts on lakes and reservoirs and you must take advantage of them, all the time. Never get to the lay-line too early, we shall cover this later in the subject of tactics.

(c) Tiller movement either side of the centre line is small so as not to slow the boat down, and they go along 'snouting' for the wind all the time.

2. Sea sailing

Sea sailors do none of the above; in fact, their course of action is the opposite.

(a) They aim for speed over the water and compromise on pointing ability. To achieve this, they sail with more upper main and jib leach twist so as to create acceleration. Twist creates speed, not pointing ability.

(b) They spend maybe only 40% of the time looking at tell-tales and more time watching the waves approaching the weather side of the boat, so as to work the boat through the waves.

(c) They use much more tiller movement to work the boat through the waves—the lighter and shorter the boat, the more effective this is.

(d) They do not spend time looking for shifts as these tend to be less frequent generally (refer to Chapter 5. *Tactics*), but instead watch the compass for a possible wind bend (see Chapter 1. *Preparation: geographical and tidal preparations*).

Holding Your Position

An important factor in boat handling is to learn to stop your boat 'dead', and to learn how long it takes to accelerate in the various wind strengths and sea states. When you have nothing better to do (e.g. in the starting area when all other checks are completed), go to a fixed object—not something floating along!—and see how long you can stay alongside it without moving away. You should be able to stay there for as long as you wish, by trimming both main and jib, centreboard, boat balance and tiller movement.

The ability to do this will give you more confidence on a starting line. Learning the characteristics of your boat is important, and the difference between classes is very significant.

Body Movement

The use of the upper body whilst sitting on the gunwale during racing on the open sea is very important and numerous articles have been written about 'Kinetic sailing'. My only message on this subject is—yes, use it, but be very careful not to infringe Rule 60.

This covers the basic points in boat handling. As said previously, you may have the fastest machine on the water, but if you cannot handle it properly, you are not going to win. Undoubtedly, effective boat handling plays a major role in the sport, but again, this alone does not win races!

3
Boat Tuning

The subject of tuning and setting up a boat correctly for the conditions of the day can be rather complex and the larger and more complicated the boat, the more variables involved and the longer it will take to evaluate all these variables.

The only way to find out what makes your boat 'tick' in all conditions is by spending many hours in that particular boat. Theory is no substitute for practical study and evaluation. Each type of boat has its own character and its own peculiarities. You may learn all there is to know about setting up your boat and making it go fast, then move into another class and expect the same rules to apply. They might, but the likelihood is that they will not. So each time you change your boat, you must start all over again and learn to know and understand your particular boat.

Sometimes too much emphasis is put on the subject of boat tuning. Some sailors get too worked up about the sails or the spars, worry about speed and pointing ability and forget everything else, failing to look at a race as a whole.

On the day, if the boat feels and looks alright forget the rig and get on with the race. But do not forget to adjust the rig as the wind strength and sea state change.

This section looks at the subject of boat tuning generally, without reference to a particular type of boat. Look at your type of boat and apply the following concepts as far as you can within your own class rules.

BOAT TUNING CONTROLS

There are ten main boat tuning controls. Your type of boat may have all ten controls or only a few, but most are available to the majority of modern racing dinghies.

First let us look at these controls as a group and establish what they are there to achieve, then we shall look at each one in more detail.

1. *Mast rake adjustment* (Plates 19 and 20 *see page 30*)
This controls the C of E of the whole rig in relation to the C of LR which affects:

- mainsail camber
- mainsail leach shape
- mast bend
- boat speed
- pointing ability
- weather and lee helm

Plate 19 *above.* Mast upright and vertical in the boat, or even slightly forward of the vertical, would be better in these light winds on the open sea.

Plate 21 *above.* Note the long spreaders stiffening the mast athwartships, to improve pointing ability.

2. *Spreaders* (Plate 21 *see page 30*)

These control the mast bend fore and aft and athwartships which affects:

- mainsail camber
- mainsail leach shape
- attacking angle of mainsail luff to the wind
- pointing ability
- boat speed

3. *Cunningham hole*

This controls the C of E of the sail which affects:

- mainsail leach shape
- pointing ability
- boat speed

Plate 20 *left.* Mast rake increased as the wind increases, so as to improve boat speed and to depower the rig.

Plate 22 (a). The kicking strap is eased a little to give upper leach twist to create speed over the waves.

Plate 22 (b). If over-powered on a reach as is the case here, ease the kicker to assist in bringing the boat back to better balance.

4. *Mast ram*
This controls mast bend fore and aft especially in the lower third which affects:

- mainsail camber
- attacking angle of mainsail luff to the wind
- mainsail leach shape
- pointing ability
- boat speed

5. *Kicking strap* (Plate 22 *see this and following page*)
This controls the mainsail leach shape which affects:

- pointing ability
- boat speed
- mast bend (throughout)
- power in the rig (especially off the wind)

6. *Barber haulers* (Plate 23 *see page 33*)
These control the slot shape between the jib leach and mainsail luff which affects:

- pointing ability
- boat speed
- attacking angle of jib to the wind
- fullness and power in the jib

7. *Traveller*
This controls the attacking angle of mainsail to the wind which affects:

- mainsail leach shape
- mast bend

8. *Centreboard adjustment*
This controls the C of LR which affects:

- pointing ability

Plate 22 (c) *above*. The three boats to the left have too much mainsail leach twist on flat water. They require more kicker tension as in the 470–K472, to improve pointing ability.

Plate 22 (d) *below*. The boat to windward has not enough kicker tension and too much leach twist, whereas the boat to leeward has too much kicker tension and not enough twist.

Plate 23 (a) *above*. Slot shape too narrow, thereby stalling the wind passing around the leeward side of the mainsail.

Plate 23 (b) *below*. Slot shape too open, therefore not accelerating the wind around the leeward side of the main.

Plate 23 (c) *above*. Slot shape correct, producing good speed and pointing ability.

- boat speed
- boat balance

9. *Main clew outhaul* (Plate 24 *see page 34*)
This controls the mainsail camber (especially the lower third), which affects:

- mainsail leach shape
- pointing ability
- boat speed

10. *Spinnaker pole adjustment* (Plate 25 *see page 34*)
This controls the spinnaker slot shape, which affects:

- boat speed
- spinnaker twist

Before looking at these various tuning controls and actually setting your boat up,

Plate 24 (a). Main clew outhaul eased to create more fullness and power, but over-hooking the leach which is stalling the wind, creating drag off the leach. This is indicated by the tell-tales which are not streaming off the leach.

Plate 24 (b). Pulling the clew outhaul further outboard assists the leach to open and prevents stalling and drag as indicated by the tell-tales now streaming off the leach.

do not forget that you must take into consideration the following factors:

Wind strength
Sea state
All-up crew weight
Basic sail shape

Also, remember another basic theory:

Flat or short choppy water—
    flatter sails—harder leaches
Choppy water—fuller sails—
    more twist

Mast Rake Adjustment

Controls to adjust mast rake are available in most three sail, high-performance dinghies. If they are not, the mast rake must be set up for the conditions of the day in the dinghy park before going afloat.

When we talk about mast rake, we are talking about moving the truck of the mast fore and aft and not about moving the heel of the mast. So what does this achieve and what are we looking for?

The wind strength is the deciding factor for the position of the mast. Let us consider two extremes:

1. *Light winds on the open sea* (Plate 26)
The mast should be almost vertical in the boat or slightly forward of the vertical in these conditions (Fig 2 *see page 36*).

With the mast in this position we are achieving the following:

• with all three corners of the mainsail in equal tension, a full, more powerful mainsail with maximum camber;
• a mainsail leach which will more readily stand up to windward;

Plate 25 *opposite*. The spinnaker pole height must be adjusted so that the two corners are the same height above the water. The pole is too high in 420-36532, and correct in 40218.

• the C of E of the whole rig will be brought more directly above the C of LR and maybe slightly forward of it.

Creating mainsail leach twist for acceleration and speed will be covered later under the use of a traveller. However, it is relevant to mention at this stage that you acquire speed and acceleration out of leach twist and pointing ability from a leach which hooks to windward. You must know which to acquire for the conditions of the day, but as a general

Plate 26. A full, powerful mainsail with a hooking leach. Fullness and power are only required on the open sea in light winds. You need leach twist and not a hooking leach.

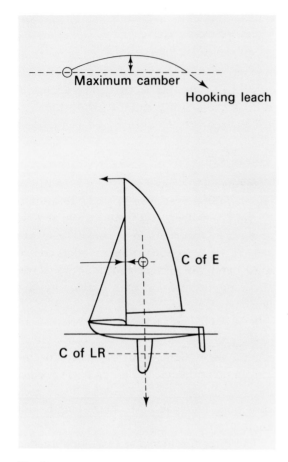

Fig. 2.
Mast vertical or slightly forward. Good for light winds on the open sea, sloppy water. Boom end slightly above the horizontal. The traveller must be used to create mainsail leach twist.

Fig. 3.
Increase the mast rake to induce leach twist, giving a flatter mainsail and a wider slot shape to depower the rig.

rule, open sea and choppy conditions require twist for speed, and flat water requires harder leaches for pointing ability.

2. *Medium to strong winds on the open sea* (Plate 27)

(Applicable to most high performance dinghies, but not all.) As the wind increases, you will slowly but surely become over-powered. This can be reduced by increasing mast rake (Fig. 3). You may think that this will increase weather helm, but it does not. If the whole mast is moved further aft in the boat, then it would. By moving only the truck aft, we reduce the height of the mast head and hounds to the deck. This allows the following:

• the mast bends more readily at spreader height, forward and to windward, which creates upper mainsail leach twist and jib leach twist;

Plate 27. Increased mast rake to assist in flattening the mainsail (mast bend forward), and open/twist the upper mainsail leach to reduce the heeling moment of the boat and increase speed over the water, compromising on pointing ability.

• the heeling moment of the boat is reduced and therefore increases speed and acceleration;

• the pointing ability is reduced, which is less important in these stronger winds when boat balance and speed over the water are more vital;

• a flatter mainsail is acquired which depowers the rig and results in a more vertical mainsail leach throughout.

Increased mast rake should be adopted in the medium to stronger winds on the open sea and on flat water; and also in light winds on flat water. In allowing the rig to go aft further, so does the C of E in relation to the C of LR, but this is compensated for by raising the board a little bringing the C of LR back below the C of E.

Spreaders

Spreaders are a most important boat tuning control, often overlooked by a large number of dinghy sailors. Both the length and the angle are important in whatever boat you sail (Fig. 4 *see page 38*). The spreaders control mast bend fore and aft and sideways as well as being critical for pointing ability and power in the rig.

If you sail a class of boat where you are tied to one suit of sails or are restricted by regatta regulations, you may need to alter the length and angle of the spreaders to meet the conditions of the day, by having spreaders adjustable in both length and angle.

The three traditional settings for spreaders are long, standard and short spreaders, as follows:

LONG SPREADERS (Plate 28 *see pages 39–40*)

Long spreaders deflect the shrouds outboard as you look up from the chain plate to the hounds. When this rig is put under tension, the mast is supported sideways and is stiffened up so that there is no bend either to leeward or to windward.

This will improve pointing ability and is very effective, but can only be done in boats with small overlapping jibs as in, for example, the Soling, Star, 505, 470, 420, Fireball, etc.

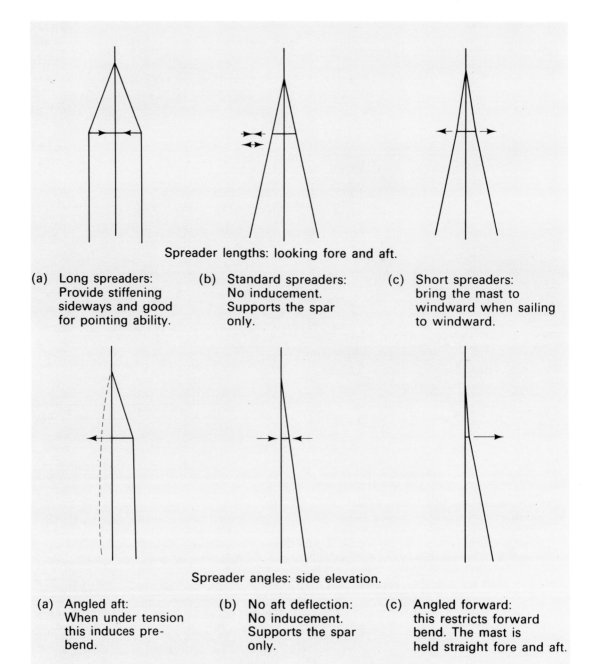

Spreader lengths: looking fore and aft.

(a) Long spreaders:
Provide stiffening
sideways and good
for pointing ability.

(b) Standard spreaders:
No inducement.
Supports the spar
only.

(c) Short spreaders:
bring the mast to
windward when sailing
to windward.

Spreader angles: side elevation.

(a) Angled aft:
When under tension
this induces pre-
bend.

(b) No aft deflection:
No inducement.
Supports the spar
only.

(c) Angled forward:
this restricts forward
bend. The mast is
held straight fore and aft.

Fig. 4.
Spreader lengths and angles.

Plate 28. (a) *above*. At the start of this race three boats, 348, 351 and 342 are very close together.

Plate 28. (b) *below*. Two to three minutes after the start, the mainsail leach twist and shape of 351 and 342 (right and middle) are almost identical–controlled by spreader length and angle combined with mainsheet and kicker tension. 348 has much more leach twist.

Plate 28 (c). 348 (later on in the race), has too much mast bend forward, allowing too much leach twist in both the jib and mainsail. The spreaders should be angled slightly further forward, so as to put more power back into the whole rig.

Plate 28 (d). 342 (same day)–how it should look!

If these spreaders are angled aft—looking up from the chain plates to the hounds—shrouds are now deflected aft as well as outboard. When the rig is put in tension, the mast is supported sideways still, but it is also pushed forward at spreader height. This is what is commonly called pre-bending the mast. You do this to achieve the following:

- create a finer entry into the mast with the mainsail luff;
- create a flatter mainsail;
- create upper mainsail leach twist.

It is important to have this set up when sailing on flat water or short choppy water, in any wind range. Make sure though that the mainsail has enough luff curve built into it to take the bend, otherwise the mainsail will be too flat with too much upper leach twist, which in turn will make you underpowered and you will lose your pointing ability. This will be obvious to you not only because others will sail past you pointing higher, but also by creases forming from spreaders to clew across the bias of the cloth.

STANDARD SPREADERS

Looking up from chain plate to the hounds, rig in tension, there is no deflection of the shrouds in any direction—nothing is being achieved. All we are doing is supporting the mast and not making it do anything with regard to matching it to our mainsail for conditions of the day. While sailing you will, if anything, be restricting the mast from going forward and maybe bringing it to windward slightly. This is perhaps a good position from which to start before adjusting to match spar and sail together for the prevailing conditions.

In the case of short spreaders, with the rig in tension looking up the shrouds, there is now deflection inboard before reaching the hounds. In this situation, with the boat sailing to windward you are now inducing the mast to come up to windward at spreader height and fall off to leeward at the top.

You would want to do this in medium to stronger winds in any boat with a large overlapping genoa, so as to create a wider slot shape whilst sailing to windward and not affect pointing ability and speed through the water with a flogging mainsail. Also, if you were now to angle these spreaders further forward, you would assist in maintaining a straighter mast fore and aft, which you may have to do if using a mainsail with little or no luff curve built into it. Similarly, if you want forward bend, allow the spreader to be angled further aft to take out the fullness in the mainsail and depower the rig, creating

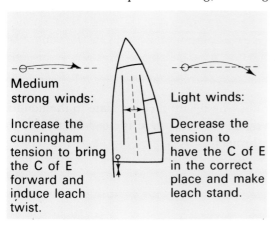

Medium strong winds:

Increase the cunningham tension to bring the C of E forward and induce leach twist.

Light winds:

Decrease the tension to have the C of E in the correct place and make leach stand.

Fig. 5.
Use of the cunningham hole.

upper mainsail leach twist for speed and acceleration.

It is important with the three traditional settings for spreaders to make sure that the outboard end bisects the angle to the shroud equally so that it is not too high or too low at the outboard end.

Cunningham Hole

The cunningham hole is designed to control the C of E of a sail and not to flatten it as some people like to believe, although it may give this effect (Fig. 5).

The C of E is built into a sail approximately 45–50% back from its leading edge. As the wind increases over the aerofoil shape, the C of E is forced back in the sail to approximately 65–75% aft of its leading edge. Once this happens the leach of the sail wants to hook up to windward more, stalling the wind trying to exhaust off the leach, and increasing the heeling moment and weather helm of the boat. You are in effect gaining pointing ability but losing out on speed over the water, which in these conditions is more important.

So, as the wind increases, the cunningham hole tension should bring the C of E of the sail back to where it belongs, as designed by the sailmaker. As the wind increases even more, the cunningham hole tension should also increase, in order to keep the C of E well forward in the sail. This will have the effect of opening the leach of the sail, especially in the upper half, and reducing the heeling moment of the boat, creating acceleration and speed. The softer the cloth, the more effective this is down the length of the leach.

Mast Ram

The use of this control is very important with regard to the power in the mainsail and the shape of the mainsail leach.

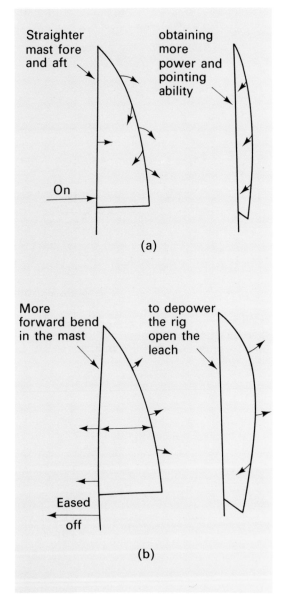

Fig. 6.
Use of mast ram-chocks.

By keeping the mast ram on, (Fig. 6(a)) and keeping a straight spar fore and aft, more camber is put back into the sail and therefore the mainsail leach wants to hook up to windward. Also the attacking angle of the mainsail luff to the wind is widened. This should be achieved on the open sea in light to medium winds, but so as not to close the mainsail leach. You now need to use the traveller (but should have no kicking strap tension) in order to keep enough mainsail leach twist.

By easing the mast ram, (Fig. 6(b)) obviously the reverse is going to be achieved. You will now start to depower the mainsail by creating a flatter sail and opening the mainsail leach from the top to approximately mid-height. At the same time you will create a narrower angle of attack of the mainsail luff into the mast and into the wind. You would want to achieve this in medium to strong winds in any sea state, and possibly in light winds on flat water, in the majority of classes.

The mast ram is a critical boat tuning control and it is very important to relate it to the conditions of the day and the all-up weight in the boat. There is one final consideration with a mast ram depending on the type of spar being used (softness fore and aft). On the open sea in light winds, leave the ram off so that as the boat pitches, the mast works with the boat and does not shake the sails too much, disturbing the airflow.

Kicking Strap

The kicking strap or kicker is one of, if not *the* most important boat tuning control. You must fully appreciate what you are doing when either tightening, or easing it off (Fig. 7). Many sailors tension it and leave it at that for the whole of the race. This is definitely not the thing to do!

When tensioning the kicking strap the following points must be considered:

Fig. 7. (right)
Kicking Strap. Tensioned and eased.

1. How are you affecting the mainsail leach shape?
2. How much are you going to bend the mast?

The kicking strap alone is responsible for:

• pointing ability,
• speed over the water,
• power in the rig,
• broaching and/or capsizing.

While racing to windward and reaching, the best visual means of checking the mainsail leach shape is to have two tell-tales, one just below the top batten and the other at mid-height. More than this can be worrying! You must keep these tell-tales streaming horizontally off the leach. If they break down and go round to leeward of the leach, you have too much kicker tension and the mainsail leach hooks up to windward too much. The opposite happens if the tell-tales are streaming upwards off the leach, you then have too much twist in the sail.

Remember, twist gives speed, and hooking gives pointing ability and less speed. Use the kicker for powering and depowering the rig off the wind in various wind strengths.

Barber Haulers

A barber hauler (Fig. 8 *see page 44*) is the piece of kit which is designed to control the exact position of the clew of the headsail both inboard and outboard, and up and down. This is also a critical boat tuning control affecting both speed and pointing ability.

It controls the slot shape (the area between the headsail leach and the luff area of the

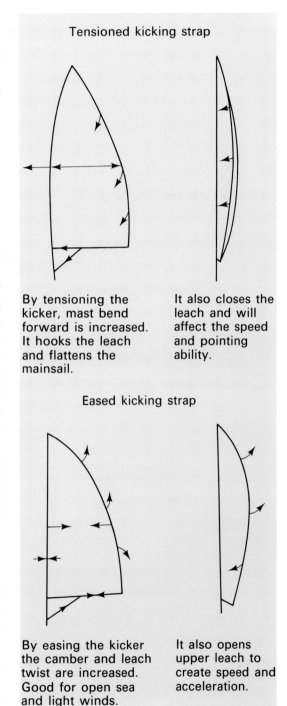

Tensioned kicking strap

By tensioning the kicker, mast bend forward is increased. It hooks the leach and flattens the mainsail.

It also closes the leach and will affect the speed and pointing ability.

Eased kicking strap

By easing the kicker the camber and leach twist are increased. Good for open sea and light winds.

It also opens upper leach to create speed and acceleration.

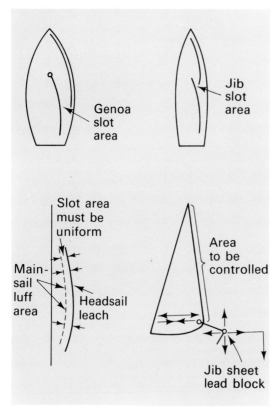

Fig. 8.
Barber haulers. The slot shape must be adjusted with a change in the wind strength and sea state.

mainsail). Too much twist will create speed but pointing ability will be poor. A hooking jib leach will create pointing ability but reduce speed over the water, so a compromise must be reached for the various wind strengths and sea states.

Your best visual indication that the slot shape is correct whilst racing is that the luff area of the mainsail should be just thinking about lifting and/or backwinding. If it is excessive, the slot width and shape is too narrow and if there is no indication of lifting, it is probably too open.

Other basic points about this critical slot area are:

- light winds, flat water—narrow slot
- sloppy water—slightly more open with more upper jib leach twist
- medium wind range—uniform even slot throughout
- strong winds—wider slot with twist.

All racing machines with high aspect ratio jibs, (such as Soling, Star, Etchell, Fireball, 420, 470 and 505) carry their jib with a narrow angle of attack to the wind all the time and control the fullness and leach shape from this inboard sheeting position. In boats with large overlapping genoas (such as the Dragon, Flying Dutchman and GP14), control of the slot area is mainly in the vertical plane but may also be inboard or outboard on a track too.

With the clew of a headsail being controlled in this way, not only is the leach shape controlled, but also the shape of the sail, i.e. the fullness. On the open sea, more fullness and twist is the golden rule for speed over the course, whereas on flat water, a flatter sail and harder leach is normally preferred to achieve both speed and pointing ability.

It is also important to remember that your jib sheets must be marked and calibrated so as to achieve the correct slot shape in all sea and wind conditions.

Traveller

This control is used in combination with the kicking strap, main clew outhaul and mainsheet tension (Fig. 9). The traveller is used, for the most part, to control the mainsail leach shape, in conjunction with the mainsheet. There are basically three positions for the traveller to achieve the required leach shape:

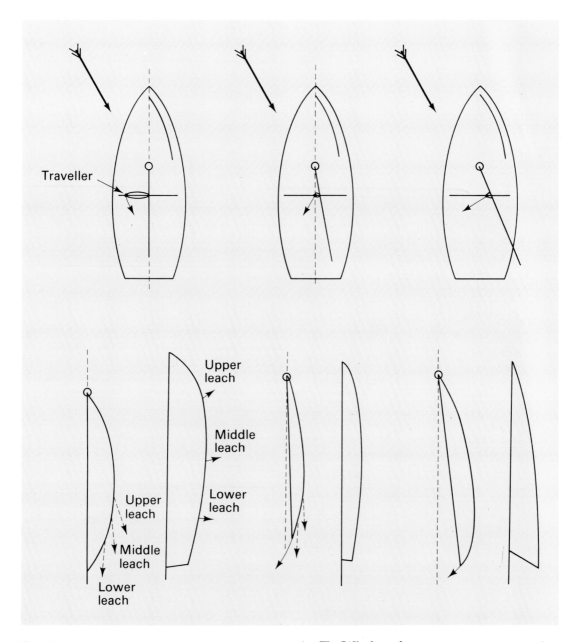

Fig. 9.

- to windward
- centre
- to leeward

1. *To Windward*

Light winds and open sea. Whilst racing to windward in these conditions, in order to keep the boom on or near the centreline, you will require little mainsheet tension with the traveller to windward, therefore putting minimum load down the mainsail leach. With the kicker off, you are now inducing mainsail leach twist which is required in these conditions with a full mainsail for maximum speed over the sloppy water. In larger boats fitted with bar kicking straps, reverse the thrust to induce mainsail leach twist.

2. *Centre*

Medium wind range, on the sea or flat water. As you move into the medium wind range, you now look for maximum power in the rig, speed and pointing ability. The traveller must be on the centreline to achieve this, otherwise you will begin to lose pointing ability if sailing to windward, and power whilst reaching and running.

3. *To leeward*

Strong winds and flat water. This is the only time to have the traveller in this position because, to keep the boom over the quarter of the boat, you will require a lot of mainsheet tension. With the traveller in this position you achieve the following:

- bend the mast and flatten the sail fore and aft;
- bend the mast to windward at mid-height and to leeward at the top, creating upper leach twist and closing the leach in the lower half for pointing ability.

Having the kicker on relatively hard is good for both speed and pointing ability in strong winds on flat water, and/or on short choppy water. With the traveller in the leeward position and with a harder leach in the lower section, stalling of the wind trying to escape off the leach and increased weather helm are not experienced. This is only applicable to boats with high aspect ratio jibs and singlehanders. With a boat with a large overlapping genoa in a strong breeze, you cannot let the traveller off to leeward as you will be choking the slot area.

Centreboard Adjustment

It has already been emphasised that the centreboard is a vital control affecting boat balance, weather helm, leeway, etc. and the adjustment of the board is critical in boat-handling and tuning. *Do not forget it!*

DOUBLEHANDERS

1. *Racing to windward in light winds*
Get the bottom leading corner of the centreboard forward of the vertical (within class rules) so that when you trim the boat by the bow, the leading edge in fact becomes vertical, which improves pointing ability.

2. *Racing to windward in strong winds*
Having depowered the rig, raise the centreboard a little to assist boat balance and reduce weather helm.

3. *Reaching in strong winds*
Use less centreboard to assist boat balance and reduce the risk of broaching. This will also allow you to bear away with less pressure on the rudder blade and reduce the risk of stalling.

Note: If you have large self-bailers, close one of them, otherwise the turbulence created by them will assist in stalling the rudder blade!

SINGLEHANDERS

The above three points apply to single-handed racing (using a daggerboard) as well as doublehanded racing. In addition, when over-powered to windward on the open sea in choppy water, the daggerboard should be raised two–three inches. On flat water, keep the board down and feather the boat into the wind more to spill the wind and pinch the boat. Go for pointing ability and less for speed in these conditions.

USE OF CENTREBOARD OR DAGGERBOARD
WHILST ROUNDING MARKS IN STRONG WINDS

1. *Windward Mark*
• Doublehanders: lower the centreboard prior to rounding the mark.
  enough so as not to broach whilst hoisting the spinnaker.
• Singlehanders: raise the daggerboard prior to rounding the windward mark as you approach it, so as to enable you to bear away without broaching and with the least amount of tiller movement to windward.

2. *Leeward Mark*
• Doublehanders: lower the centreboard prior to rounding the mark.
• Singlehanders: lower the daggerboard on completion of rounding the mark. This reduces the risk of broaching and running into the mark, and/or passing to windward of it. This applies only in medium to strong winds, and can be lowered before the rounding in the light to medium wind range.

Main Clew Outhaul

The main clew outhaul is another vital boat tuning control often forgotten by a large number of sailors!

The position of the main clew outhaul must change on all basic points of sailing and changes of wind strength. It controls the power in the sail, pointing ability and speed over the water. By moving this point of the sail only a couple of inches (depending on the size of the mainsail area), you can create a drastic effect on the mainsail camber and mainsail leach shape. It is important to remember what is happening to the sail as you move the position of the clew. As you tension the clew outhaul, you start to flatten the sail and open the leach, and vice versa as you decrease the tension.

The need to achieve either of these situations varies from class to class depending on the shape of the mainsail (height and width) as well as the depth of camber built into the sail and the built-in leach shape.

The following gives an indication of when to increase or decrease the tension of the main clew outhaul:

1. To windward—tension clew outhaul: flat water, any wind strength.
2. To windward—decrease tension: open sea, light to medium winds, but maintain leach twist with the traveller.
3. Reaching—decrease tension: light to winds for more power.
4. Running—decrease tension: light to medium winds.

(3. and 4.—the tension can be increased in strong winds.)

Spinnaker Pole Adjustment

The outboard end of the pole must be adjustable in height, so as to keep the two corners of the sail the same height above the water. Ideally the inboard end should be adjustable too, so as to keep the pole horizontal, keeping the tack of the sail as far away from the headsail as possible, when on a reach.

Spinnaker pole adjustment is more critical with boats with short poles, when the tack is already close to the headsail luff and, by raising or lowering the outboard end of the pole only, the tack is too close to the headsail luff, again on the reaching legs. It is not so critical when the pole is long enough not to have this effect.

The basic points to remember with spinnaker pole adjustment are as follows:

1. Always try to keep the two corners of the sail the same height above the water so as not to present the spinnaker twisted to the wind.
2. As the wind increases, so should the pole height, and decrease as it decreases.
3. As you balance the boat to windward or to leeward reaching or running, you are altering the height of the two corners of the sail and should adjust the height of the pole accordingly.
4. If you have excessive backwinding of the mainsail whilst reaching, raise the pole a little to create a wider slot between the spinnaker leach and the leeward side of the mainsail.

Rig Tension

This obviously varies from class to class depending on the rig, whether it is a high performance boat, the all-up crew weight, one sail or two sails, size of mainsail and jib in relation to each other, etc. For most types of boats the rule is:

- Flat water/short chop—tight rigs, shrouds and jib luff in any wind strength.
- Choppy/sloppy water—softer rigs, shrouds and jib luff in any wind range.

Also remember to change the rig tension as the conditions change (sea state and wind strength).

4
Starting

Generally speaking, a good start accounts for approximately 20–80% of the eventual success in a race. The start depends on the venue, the course and whether the race is held on a lake or on the sea. Starting well on a lake accounts for a 20% success rate and on the sea, 80%.

A good start and the first windward leg after the start are crucial in modern yacht and dinghy racing on Olympic courses. All things being equal, the race then becomes a 'procession' and the pattern is set (Plate 29 *see this and following pages*).

Plate 29 (a). A good example of a port tack start. Note the sag in the middle of the line.

Plate 29 (b) *above*. Port biased line again.

Plate 29 (c) *below*. A good start by 58068 and 51546. The others are in a lee-bow situation or out of the photograph behind the line.

Plate 29 (d) *above*. Boats over the line at both ends, and note again the sag in the middle of the line.

Plate 29 (e) *below*. Gate start. Pass close to the gate launch, at speed with no boat under your lee-bow and in clear air. A good start by boats on the right of the group and by 3039 and 2993, but the remainder have made a poor start.

Fixed Line Start

There are two types of start in a race; the fixed line start and the gate start. Let us deal with fixed line starting first. Consider the following points before making your decision as to where to start:

1. Which side of the the beat do I want to be?
2. Which will be the favoured tack off the line?
3. Is it imperative that I win this race and so must I go for the best starting position?
4. Which is the favoured end?

Once you have analysed this situation, you must then position yourself on the line bearing in mind the following:

• you want to get to either the left or right side first;
• or you can be the first to get on to port tack and cross any starboard tack boats;
• or start at the wrong end of the line so to be first to the correct side of the course;
• start in the middle looking for a conservative position tactically and work the shifts up the middle.

It does not always pay to be the pin end boat at the port end off the line unless you are in a position tactically to cross the fleet on a heavily biased port end line, or want to be amongst the leaders heading to the correct side of the course, in this case the port side.

Having said this, I feel that the 80% weighting for a good start, does apply on the open sea at major events with large fleets, but I do not think that it applies on lakes and reservoirs where there are frequent wind shifts.

There are a number of points to be noted with the fixed line start. These are listed below and will then be looked at in more detail.

1. Pick the correct end of the line to start from.
2. Do not arrive too early.
3. Create space to leeward.
4. Consider making a late port tack approach.
5. Cross the line at speed.
6. Do not get overrun to windward.
7. Stand on until clear of the starting area.
8. Use a transit.

PICK THE CORRECT END OF THE LINE TO START FROM

This can be done using four methods:

(a) Put the boat in the middle of the line head to wind (Fig. 10 (a)). The end of the line forward of the beam is the correct end to start from.

(b) Sail parallel to the line—mainsail trimmed correctly—and tack without moving the mainsheet, and sail the reciprocal course (Fig. 10 (b)). If the mainsail is luffing, you are sailing towards the correct end to start from, if the sail is over-sheeted, that is too far in and you are sailing away from the correct end to start from.

(c) Use a compass (Fig. 10 (c)). This is the most accurate way of selecting the correct end of the line, especially when the starting line is long and large fleets are racing. With the compass, line up the Outer Distance Mark and the mainmast of the committee boat.

Taking this reading to be, for example, 090°, place your boat in the middle of the line head to wind. Assume the reading for the wind is 010°, the angular difference between 010° and 090° is 080°, therefore the starboard end of the line is 010° biased towards the wind and is the correct end to start from. It is important to use a compass which is clear to read and heavily dampened so that the compass card is not badly affected by the motion of the boat.

(d) Another method is knowing the line reading and your tacking angle for the conditions of the day (Fig. 10 (d) *see page 54*). Put yourself on starboard tack off the line plus tacking angle = wind direction, similarly on port tack minus tacking angle = wind direction.

Methods (a) and (b) are good for short starting lines; (c) and (d) for long lines.

DO NOT ARRIVE TOO EARLY

It is very important to judge the speed of approach to the line. If you arrive too early you have to slow down, maybe stop and even sail backwards, which is the last thing you want to be doing at this time! Look out for Rules 37 and 40 at this stage.

CREATE SPACE TO LEEWARD

In the final seconds to the start, it is crucial to work at creating a gap to leeward so that you can bear away and accelerate at start time without having someone under your lee-bow giving you 'dirty wind'. If you are in this situation off the line, you will shoot

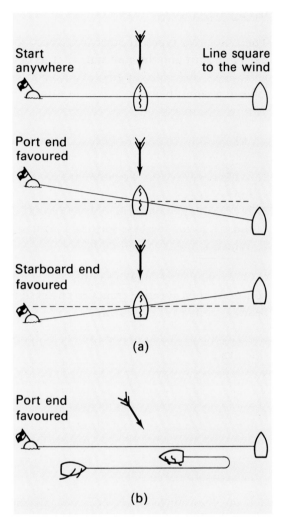

Fig. 10.
Selecting the correct end of a fixed starting line.

out backwards as the rest of the fleet passes on either side! So, it is important to create this space for yourself. One way to achieve this is to make a late port tack approach to the line.

CONSIDER MAKING A LATE PORT TACK APPROACH

There is a lot to be said for making this final

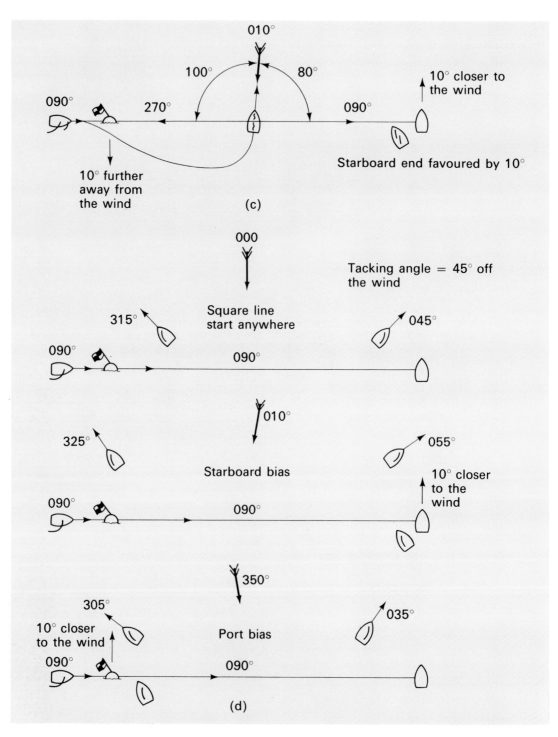

Fig. 10. (*cont.*)
Selecting the correct end of a fixed starting line.

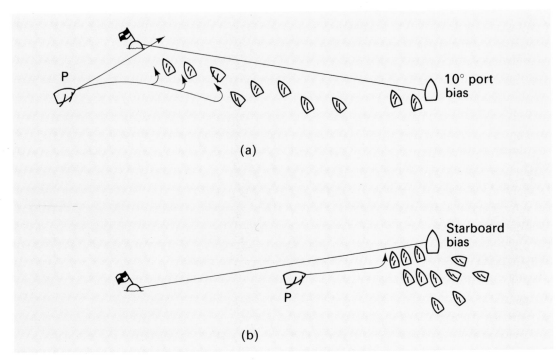

(a)

(b)

Fig. 11.

(a) *P* (port tack boat) can make a port tack start or can slot herself into a created space during the last thirty seconds.

(b) *P* is sailing along the start line on port and can now position herself to leeward of the bunch during the last thirty seconds, and make a good start in clear wind at speed.

port tack approach during the last thirty seconds as it gives you much more freedom of movement and less hassle with other boats during the final build up (Fig. 11), (Plate 30 *see page 56*). You can approach the starboard tackers, putting yourself under the opposition's lee-bow at the correct moment, and develop space to leeward. This manoeurve is also effective on heavily port-biased line—probably more so. Be careful with Rules 36, 37, 40 and 41.

A port tack approach along the line with a starboard end bias can also definitely pay off. Again, with a minute to go and the majority of the fleet hovering on starboard around the committee boat (all infringing Rule 37, 40 and 42.4s) you can idle along on port tack away from all the other boats and place yourself to leeward of the main bunch. You are now in a position to control the group of boats on your weather side using both Rules 37.1, and 40, squeezing them all up and creating a space to leeward at the same time. At start time you will lead the fleet away from the line if you execute the manoeuvre correctly. A lot of confidence is required to do this!

CROSS THE LINE AT SPEED

It is important to be travelling at speed when crossing the start line. If you are not, you will definitely be overrun both to windward and to leeward and will be sailing in a totally confused sea and wind area. If you do end

Plate 30 *above*. No. 6 makes a port tack approach to the line and is allowed to make a port tack start. A good example of how to execute this manoeuvre.

Plate 31 *below*. No. 49739 has allowed himself to be overrun to windward. He must now look for clear wind either by tacking or by easing the sheet a little and getting clear air to leeward.

up in this situation, you must go for a clear wind position first, before considering anything else. Once in this position you can consider your strategy for recovery and consolidation.

DO NOT GET OVERRUN TO WINDWARD

To get overrun to windward is as bad if not worse, as having someone under your lee-bow. Prevent it happening! (Plate 31).

It is relatively easy to avoid this. During the final countdown, check both to windward and to leeward that you are not over the line. In the dying seconds, squeeze up to the boat on your weather side and move slightly forward. As he sheets in and

accelerates, so do you. You must learn to do this in modern racing and be fairly aggressive. It is vital to be in the right place at the right time. If you are not, you are 'dead' at the start.

Be careful of the *one* or *five* minute rule (Rule 51 and Sailing Instructions).

STAND ON UNTIL CLEAR OF THE STARTING AREA

Let us assume that you have made a reasonable start, i.e. not being fouled up by a boat to leeward or by a boat sailing over the top of you, and that ahead is a clear view of the windward leg and mark. You must stand on until clear of the starting area to windward (Fig. 12). The size of this area depends on the width of the fleet and the height of the rigs.

Fig. 12.
The boats at the port and starboard end of the starting line should use the deflected wind area to gain an advantage.

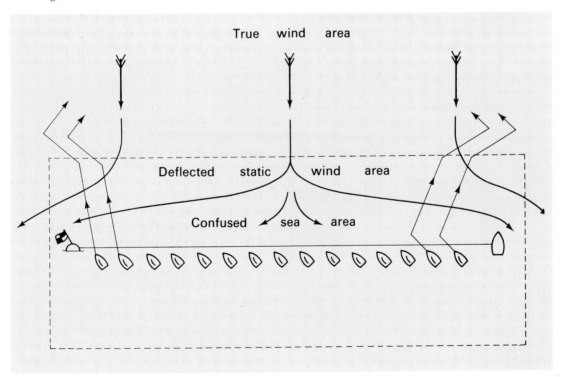

True   wind   area

Deflected   static   wind   area

Confused   sea   area

For example! If you had thirty, twelve-metre yachts on a starting line, the area of confused water and deflected wind would be quite enormous, whereas with the same number of Optimists, the area would be much smaller.

If you start at the port end of a square line, initially you may look over your shoulder and think you have been freed. You have, but only because you are being freed in the deflected wind area around the port end of the starting area. *Do not tack*—cut your losses because you are in fact gaining.

As you progress you feel that you are being headed. This is true, but only because you are leaving the deflected wind area and entering the true wind area and smoother, less confused water. You now look over your shoulder and think that now is the time to cross the fleet. How many times have we heard people say 'I could cross now', shortly after starting? This particular situation will be covered in more detail in Chapter 5 *Tactics*. The message here is, do not tack in this area of confused wind and water unless it is absolutely necessary.

USE A TRANSIT

Transits (Fig. 13) should be used whenever

Fig. 13.
Transits must be used to make a good start. Otherwise you will be either well behind or well over the line at start time. (CB = Committee Boat).

possible to enable you to judge exactly where the line is, especially if you intend to go out of the middle on a fixed start. After all, the line is not painted on the water! It is surprising how many boats in the middle of a line are either well over, or well behind at start time. Remember always to check your line and transits after the preparatory signal. (Why?—see Rule 4 (3A).)

Gate Start

In the case of a gate start, (Fig. 14 *see page 59*) you are presented with a different proposition (refer to Gate Starting Procedures in the RYA Standard Sailing Instructions). The basic questions everyone asks are: When is the best time, and where is the best place to start? (Plate 32 *see page 59*.) To answer these questions the following points must be considered:

1. Am I faster than the 'pathfinder'?
2. Which side of the beat do I want to be for the wind and the tide?
3. Or do I want to work the shifts up the middle?
4. Are we on a freeing tack out of the gate, or a heading tack?

Once you have thought about these points you will feel more confident about when to go. Other points to consider are boats to leeward and the occasional 'cowboy' trying

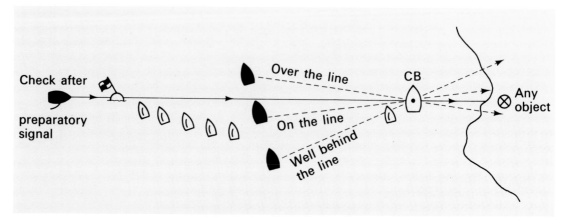

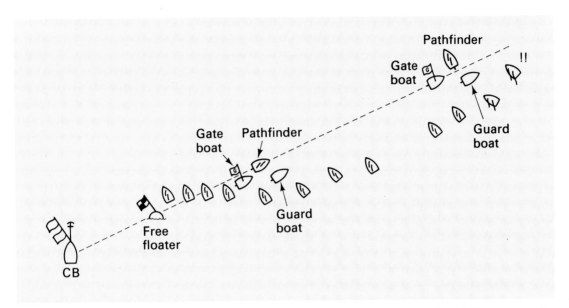

Fig. 14.
At start time, aim to pass as close as possible to the stern of the gate boat at speed, and avoid having anybody immediately to leeward of you.

Plate 32. A good gate start by K40701 at speed, close to the gate launch and with no one close to leeward.

to pass between yourself and the gate or the guard boat when there is no room for him! Finally, do not get to weather of the 'pathfinder' and find yourself having to run back to get round the guard launch or beyond the limit of the gate when it closes.

5
Tactics

The subject of tactics is a very wide one. This section will cover the main tactics which occur in every race and how you need to cope with the ever changing situations.

Overall Tactical Plan

Disregarding the tide, there are a number of points to be considered in deciding which way to go in a race area. These are as follows:

- Is there an onshore breeze?
- Is there an offshore breeze?
- Is there an oscillating breeze?
- Is there a sea breeze?
- Will the area be affected by frictional wind?
- Will the area be affected by a wind bend?

ONSHORE BREEZE

The steadiest wind with minimal oscillations occurs when the wind is blowing at right angles on to the shore (Fig. 15). The only thing that could affect this wind is the sun. With the direction of the wind initially from 170°–190° on a warm or hot day on the south coast of Britain, the wind may tend to follow the sun to the west slightly without the

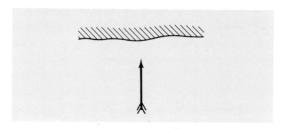

Fig. 15.
Steadiest wind direction–onshore.

sea breeze effect being there as the day gets on towards mid and late afternoon.

OFFSHORE BREEZE

If the wind is blowing offshore at right angles, the result is an oscillating wind system (Fig. 16), and the effect of this to leeward depends on the height of the land—to windward. The higher the land, the more dramatic the effect to leeward over the whole range of the racing area. The wind shifts will be more frequent in the weather mark area as well as over a wider arc, whereas in the leeward mark area the shifts will still be present, but over a narrower angle and not so frequent. It is important to avoid reaching the lay-line too early, otherwise you may find yourself easing sheets for the windward mark.

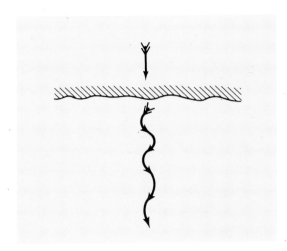

Fig. 16.
Oscillating wind–offshore: oscillations are more frequent closer to the shore.

OSCILLATING BREEZE

An oscillating breeze is one which is altering its direction around a mean wind, and is usually an offshore breeze. For example, you may have a wind direction of 030° and over a period of time have readings as follows: 030°–025°–020°–030°–035°–040°–030°–025°–etc.

The important thing to remember here is that from the starting line you must be in sequence with the shifts, always on the freeing tack and thereafter using the shifts correctly to gain maximum advantage to windward.

SEA BREEZE

This is a development which is not too frequent during the average British summer. But if you get a brilliantly sunny morning with no wind or with a slight offshore wind, these are the symptoms for the development of a sea breeze.

Go afloat to the race area and await developments, unless the Principal Race Officer is in a position to hold you ashore. The first sign of a sea breeze developing is the build-up of cumulus cloud over the land (Fig. 17(a)). This is caused by warm air rising and will shortly be followed by an inshore onshore breeze, then an onshore breeze to seaward with nothing in the middle. The cycle will soon be completed as the offshore breeze works its way into the shore and meets up with the breeze already being sucked into the land near the shore.

Fig. 17.

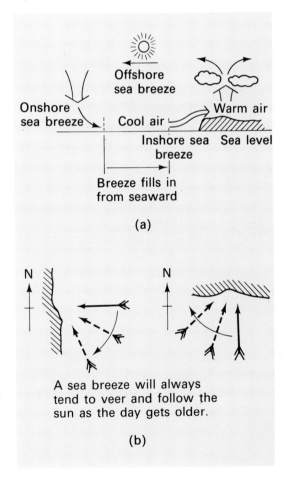

A sea breeze will always tend to veer and follow the sun as the day gets older.

(b)

Once the cycle has been completed you must now watch for it veering as the day gets older, the wind will tend to follow the sun if on the east or south coast of the UK, so watch out for the right hand side of the course (Fig. 17(b)).

FRICTIONAL WINDS

With an *onshore* breeze approaching the land at a tangent, you may feel the effect of a frictional wind, depending on the height of the land behind you and the position of the race area in relation to it. If this is the case, you must work either the left or right side of

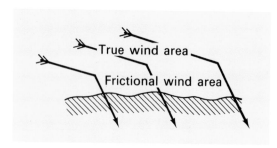

Fig. 18.
Onshore wind approaching the coastline at a tangent.

the course, depending on which side the land is (Fig. 18).

In the case of an *offshore* breeze approaching the coastline at a tangent (Fig. 19), look to windward, and if the wind is coming off a land mass on either the left or the right side of the course, that is the way you must go. This will result in your being headed as you approach the land mass, and you will then be freed on the opposite tack into the windward mark, picking up freeing shifts as you approach the mark. Do not be greedy, going too far into this frictional wind and ending up easing the sheets into the

windward mark. However, in high performance planing dinghies, this may in fact pay

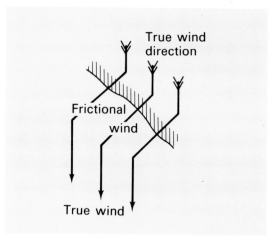

Fig. 19.
Offshore wind at a tangent. The effect to seaward of the deflected wind area depends on the height of the land and the strength of the wind.

as you approach the windward mark at speed, in clear wind.

WIND BENDS

These bends are very prominent in bays (such as Torbay and Weymouth), when the

Fig. 20.
Winds bends can be theoretically sorted out by observing land masses around the race area. Study the race area and acquire a chart or Ordnance Survey map.

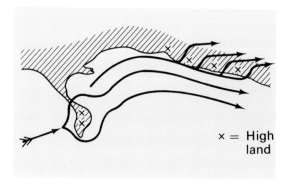

x = High land

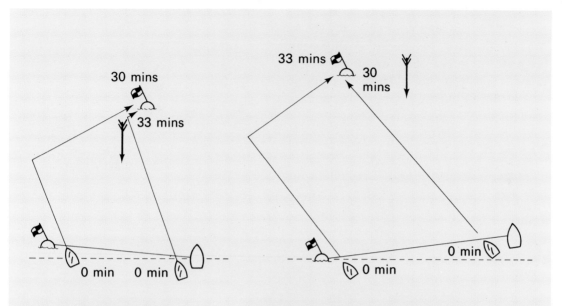

(a) Port biased line: the boat at the port end will get to the windward mark first.

(b) Starboard biased line: the starboard end boat will arrive at the windward mark first.

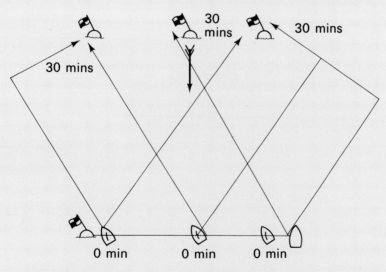

(c) Square line: start anywhere. All should arrive at the windward mark together.

Fig. 21.

wind can be channelled around a coastline guided by a high land mass (Fig. 20). These can be detected in theory during your geographical preparation as already mentioned, and you can then find them in practice by sailing the windward leg prior to the start.

Tactics in the Starting Area

These are discussed under the following headings:

- starting
- first beat
- reaching
- running.

STARTING

As already stated, it is important to consider your tactics in the starting area, and determine the most strategic position on the starting line–whether it be the port end, the starboard end or in the middle of the line.

It is totally irrelevant where the windward mark is in relation to the starting line (Fig. 21 *see page 63*). The boat starting at the correct end of a biased line, (all things being equal, tide + boat speed) will get there first. On a line which is square to the wind, it does not matter where you start from.

1. *Port end* (Fig. 22 (a))

If you want to go left and/or if this end is favoured and you can get on to port tack, cross the main bulk of the fleet before putting yourself in the middle of the field covering the fleet, or continue over to the starboard side of the beat, if that is the way to go.

2. *Starboard end* (Fig. 22 (b))

You must consider whether you wish to

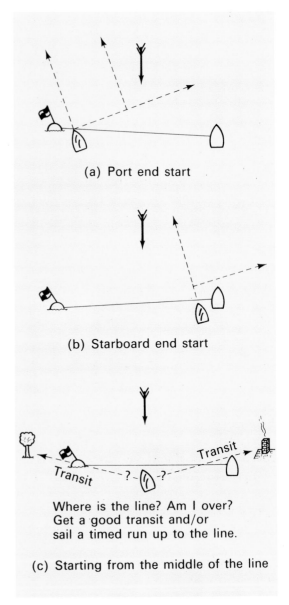

(a) Port end start

(b) Starboard end start

Where is the line? Am I over?
Get a good transit and/or
sail a timed run up to the line.

(c) Starting from the middle of the line

Fig. 22.
Tactics in the starting area.

continue on starboard tack once you have started, or whether you want to be on port tack straight away.

3. *Middle of the line* (Fig. 22 (c))

The initial problem is being near the line at the start and having a good transit to establish this, otherwise you may end up in a traditional sag to leeward.

FIRST BEAT

Let us assume that you have made a reasonable start, avoiding trouble to leeward, windward or ahead, and in front of you is the open water. What must you consider next?

1. *Boat speed*

The helmsman must concentrate on boat speed and nothing else. The amount of drive at this stage of the race is critical. Get away from the opposition as quickly as possible.

2. *Communication between helmsman and crew*

Now is the time for the crew to start communicating all useful and constructive information to the helmsman as to what is happening outside the boat, so that the helmsman can concentrate purely on the speed of the boat and the waves. This is one of the most important points about good crews who very often play a bigger role in winning races than the helmsman.

Once settled on a tack, the crew must be the eyes of the boat. Information should be flowing to the helmsman at all relevant stages, such as:

- boat is going OK/it isn't going–do something about it!
- we are pointing all right/we are not...
- if you wish to tack you are clear to do so/you are not clear...
- boat coming on port/starboard, you are/are not clear–have you seen him?

- main opposition is coming with us/has tacked off and is going the other way
- we are sailing into a header/freer
- there appears to be more/less wind here/over there
- he is tacking off/he is gybing (if in a duel).

The helmsman may or may not act on the information given, but he must have it!

3. *Keep your wind clear*

Anyone who can sail the whole of the first beat in clear wind will end up in a respectable position at the windward mark, as long as you have boat speed.

4. *Assess whether you are right*

Even though you have done your homework and are a third or two-thirds up the first beat, you must assess tactically whether or not you are going the correct way! Often you carry on in the same direction saying to yourself that it will all come good.... it will not, except in very rare instances.

Now is the time to assess the situation and if necessary admit that you are in the wrong place at the wrong time. *TACK*. Get across to the other boats, consolidate your position and work up from that point, as opposed to losing everything because you are too stubborn! Winning regattas is not about taking chances, it is about putting a consistent series together. You do not have to win a race to win a championship, though occasionally it does help if you do!

5. *Consider your tactics when approaching the windward mark* (Plate 33 see page 66)

There is much to be gained or lost at this point. Too many sailors approach the weather mark on port tack at the same time as the rest of the fleet arrives on starboard tack. It is not wrong to approach the

Plate 33 (a) *above*. Be careful in your final approach to the windward mark. Here K519 is sailing over the top of K472 who may not make the windward mark, so should consider getting out of this position.

Plate 33 (b) *below*. Be very careful about Rules 36 and 41. K38285 has to exercise great care not to infringe these rules in his final approach.

windward mark on port, but in doing so you must ensure that you are in a position to actually round it without infringing Rules 36 and 41.1. Also you do not want to put yourself in the position of having to bear away around a lot of sterns approaching on starboard, or tacking under another boat's lee-bow and then find that you are unable to lay the mark (marks to port) and have to gybe round to make a new approach.

6. *Play the windshifts, but be careful!*

For reasons already mentioned, you must exercise care in using windshifts. On lakes and reservoirs, it is important to use all the shifts but not to arrive on the lay-line too early. Whereas on the open sea, you may well be sailing into a wind bend and it would pay you to get well into it before tacking. Again you must not get on to the lay-line in this situation especially if when coming to the windward mark, the surface current is under your lee-bow! The use of either windshifts and/or windbends must be part of

your homework (see Chapter 1, geographical and tidal preparations), as well as part of your preparation on the water prior to the start.

When approaching the windward mark, marks to port, (Fig. 23) behind boats which have already rounded the mark, it will pay you to be below the lay-line on port tack, to

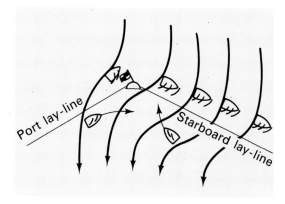

Fig. 24.
In this example, when approaching on port tack, it may pay to be above the lay-line to ensure that you get round the windward mark.

take advantage of the freeing shifts in the deflected wind area, and to be above the lay-line on starboard tack as you may be headed whilst approaching the windward mark, and vice versa when marks are to starboard (Fig. 24).

REACHING

Having reached the windward mark this is not the time to relax. You must concentrate on the following:

1. *Defend your wind*

As you round the weather mark, if you have the opposition close on your transom you must defend your wind first (Fig. 25), (Plate 34 *see page 68 for both*). As you climb, boats

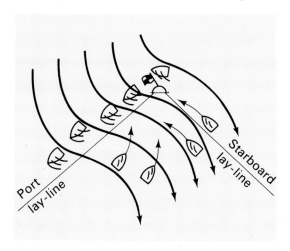

Fig. 23.
When approaching the windward mark on port, stay below the lay-line so as to be freed on port tack in the deflected wind area of the boats to windward.

Plate 34. Here the boat with no sail number must look out for K420228 about to take her wind and sail over the top of her. There is much to be lost here by the leading boat.

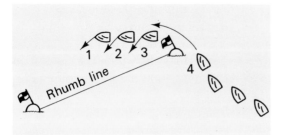

Fig. 25.
If boats 1, 2 and 3 go high initially so as to defend their wind, boat 4 should seek the advantage by sailing straight down the rhumb line if clear to do so from boats astern.

close astern will soon peel off to leeward and as they do so, so must you. If you do not, they will gain overlaps to leeward and be inside you at the gybe mark.

2. *If it is a fine reach, go high first*

If the wind backs further (marks to port), you will be between the opposition and the gybe mark, and in a position to meet the new wind as it comes through (Fig. 26), (Plate 35 *see page 69*). If the wind does not back any

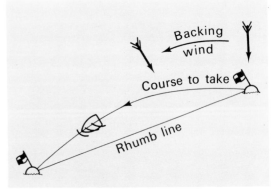

Fig. 26.
This course should be selected if there is a surface current or tide taking you from the windward side to the leeward side of the rhumb line.

more, once you get approximately half-way down the reach you can bear away, put the spinnaker up and reach into the gybe mark.

You must also go high to allow for any tide or surface current that may be taking you to leeward of the rhumb line for the mark.

3. If broad, go low first

If the wind has veered during the first beat (marks to port), you will have a broad reach, in which case, you must go low first (Fig. 27), (Plate 36 *see page 70*). This will put you in a position where again you are on the correct side of the rhumb line and if the wind should continue to veer, you will meet the new wind first. If it does not veer any more, midway down the reach you can start to luff up slightly to approach the mark on faster

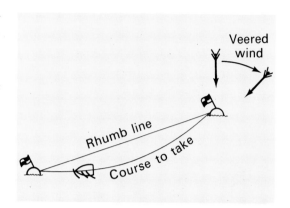

Fig. 27.
This course should be selected if the surface current or tide is taking you from the leeward side to the windward side of the rhumb line.

point of sailing, so as to gain overlaps on those boats which went too high initially down the reach and have had to gybe to get to the gybe mark.

You would also go low first to allow for any tide or surface current taking you to windward of the rhumb line for the mark.

Plate 35. 39552 climbs high above the rhumb line on this close reach in gusty conditions. Boats well to leeward of the rhumb line will find difficulty in climbing back up to the gybe mark.

Plate 36. These boats have gone low on the broad reach (windward mark out of the photograph to the left). They will come into the gybe mark sailing closer to the wind and on a faster point of sailing.

4. *Bear away to hoist the spinnaker*

If you are in a position to do so (i.e. there is no one close astern), you must bear away beyond the rhumb line for the gybe mark, and sort out and hoist the spinnaker, especially in a breeze (Fig. 28 *see page 71*), (Plate 37). If you do not hoist and set it quickly, you stand a good chance of broaching and/or capsizing with the spinnaker filling when you are not ready for it, if the centreboard is still too far down! Once you have the spinnaker sorted out and you are ready, then you can come back up to and above the rhumb line if required.

Plate 37 *right*. 41029 has borne right away, ignoring the course to the gybe mark while hoisting the spinnaker.

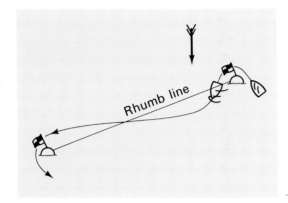

Fig. 28.
It is not necessary to head for the gybe mark whilst hoisting the spinnaker.

5. *Play the waves and gusts*

In gusty conditions, when you are 'flying' down the reach–at an altitude of three feet!–you must play both the waves and the gusts (Fig. 29), keeping the boat driving all the way down the reaching legs. Bear away and go with the gusts, and come up in the lulls to maintain the apparent wind speed and boat speed.

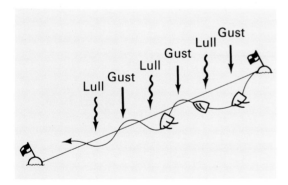

Fig. 29.

6. *Use of the kicking strap*

If you are under-powered on a reaching leg you may need:

• either a little more kicker tension;

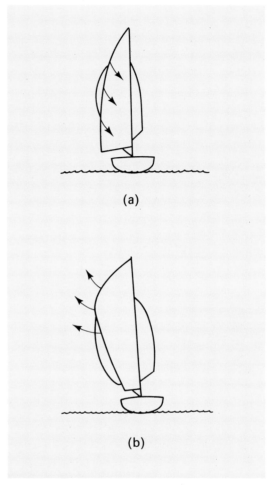

(a)

(b)

Fig.30.
(a) Tension the kicker in the medium wind range for power.
(b) Ease the kicker in strong and light winds to maintain stability and speed.

• more board down;
• or a combination of both.

If over-powered, you need the opposite.

If you are carrying three sails and are over-powered, and find that you are getting below the rhumb line, then ease the kicker and raise the board more—depending on the

Plate 38. 38169 is over-powered on a three sail reach. The helm should be sitting out further, the board brought up a little more, and the kicker eased a little to open the upper mainsail leach and reduce the heeling moment of the boat.

type of boat and its characteristics (Fig. 30), (Plate 38 *see page 72*).

The kicker can be eased all the way if necessary to open the mainsail leach and allow the wind to escape off the mainsail completely, so that the boat becomes more upright and stable with the spinnaker and jib still pulling together.

Pull the mainsheet in just to keep the lower part of the mainsail pulling. This gives you the power required to keep the boat stable and driving. The combination of kicking strap and board position is critical on the reaching legs, so you should know where to put them in your particular boat for the conditions of the day.

RUNNING

There are many things to consider on this leg so again, this is not the time to relax! If you want to gain maximum speed and advantage, consider the following:

1. *Correct gybe*
On rounding the windward mark on to a dead run and in oscillating wind conditions, you must ensure that you are on the correct gybe, otherwise you will be out of sequence

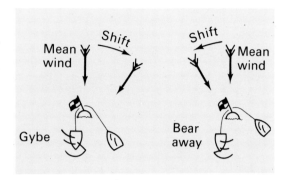

Fig. 31.
Once in sequence with the windshifts on the running leg, use your burgee to assess when to gybe as the wind shifts, so that you are not sailing by the lee.

with the shifts possibly for most of the way down the run (Fig. 31). The best way to check which gybe to be on is as follows:

- as you approach the windward mark, check the wind direction;
- if it has veered (marks to port), you must gybe straight away;
- if it has backed, just bear away.

Plate 39. 39978 and the boat to leeward have fairly good boat trim for the conditions though both could have slightly more balance to windward. The rest of the group need to work on their balance and trim for the conditions. They should be trimmed down by the bow and balanced to windward.

Plate 40 (a). Not enough kicker, too much twist in the upper leach area, causing loss of power and speed and a capsize to windward.

Plate 40 (b). More kicker tension, leach hooking too much, stalling the air flow across the sail. Needs the upper leach to be just a little more open.

It is on this running leg that the flag/windex comes into its own, using it to check windshifts, whereas when you go to windward you may not use it at all.

2. *Check your boat balance and trim*

You must check the trim of your boat during the running leg and if necessary adjust all the way down the run, if the conditions justify it (Plate 39 *see page 73*). In two-man boats in particular, the helmsman often becomes lazy and relies entirely on the crew to adjust boat trim and balance. This is not the way to win races.

3. *Use of the kicking strap*

The use of your kicking strap is very important (Plate 40). As a general rule, the stronger the wind, the more kicking strap you need—which is opposite to reaching. The tension of the kicking strap on the running leg can alone destroy boat speed and be responsible for a windward capsize. The kicker also has a dramatic effect on the mainsail, as it can take the power away or increase it. If you increase the kicker tension on a dead run in a strong blow, the mast bends to windward and flattens the mainsail. In the light to medium wind range, the

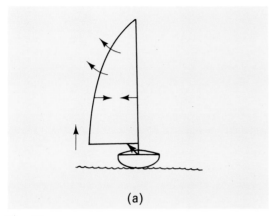

(a)

Fig. 32.
(a) Ease the kicker in light to medium winds, to maintain power and speed.

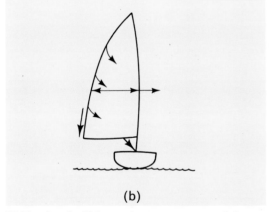

(b)

(b) Tension the kicker to decrease power, and close up the leach to reduce the risk of the death roll in strong winds.

kicker should be eased so as to put power back into the mainsail and open the upper leach for twist and acceleration (Fig. 32).

In light winds with a tight kicker, you create too hard a leach which in turn creates a situation where the wind is not allowed to escape off the leach area at all, and therefore a pocket of static wind will develop in the mainsail which will result in the loss of boat speed.

When sailing in stronger winds with the

kicker eased, the opposite effect is achieved. The wind is allowed to escape off the upper leach area, yet is retained in the lower leach area. When looking at the mainsail from a side elevation, the upper main leach is twisting forward of the mast whereas the lower area is not because of the angle of the boom from the centreline of the boat. When in this situation you are quite vulnerable to capsizing to windward. So remember, the harder it blows on a dead run, the more kicker tension you will require to eliminate leach twist and the risk of the 'death roll' and possibly capsizing to windward.

4. Adjust the spinnaker sheet leads in strong winds

If the spinnaker is set in strong winds on a dead run, the oscillations of the spinnaker can be responsible for the boat broaching and/or capsizing, and the larger the spinnaker, the more dramatic the effect.

This situation can arise when the force in the spinnaker (C of E), is initially allowed to come too far over to the windward side of the boat. This then drags the upper mast area over to windward and puts the weather bow under pressure, which in turn puts the rudder under pressure to keep the boat on a straight course. When she comes upright, the same thing happens to leeward as pressure changes from bow to bow.

With the spinnaker now oscillating from side to side, this motion will cause a broach and/or capsize (Fig. 33 see page 76). To reduce these oscillations, not only must the guy be strapped down in the shroud area, but also the sheet. If the sheet is coming from further aft, the arc of oscillation is allowed to increase, and so does the risk of the 'death roll'!

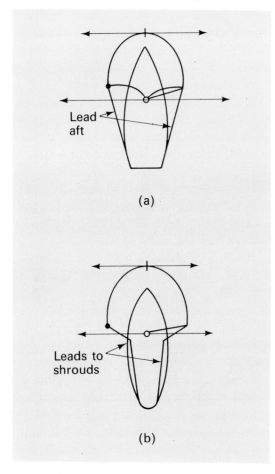

Fig. 33.
(a) With the transom sheeted, there is less control of the spinnaker and greater oscillation, which is the cause of the death roll.
(b) Strapping the spinnaker sheets down by the shrouds gives more control and reduced oscillation, and therefore less risk of the death roll.

Always remember that on a dead run in a breeze, the faster you are going the safer you are. But if the oscillation of the spinnaker—even though it has been strapped down and not allowed to go over to windward—is still causing you to broach violently and lose control, now is the time to take it down!

5. *Tactics*

As well as ensuring that you are always on the correct gybe and catching any shifts, you must tactically keep yourself between the opposition and the leeward mark. This does create problems as you must also keep your wind clear, but it can and must be done. You do not let yourself get to one side of the rhumb line whilst the opposition goes to the other, unless you have good reasons for doing so, (tidal or new wind considerations for example).

You must also think about your approach to the leeward mark. Too many sailors come into the mark at too narrow an angle, gybing alongside the mark and making a poor rounding. Ideally, your approach should be:

- on the correct gybe at a wide angle of approach with a narrow exit;
- close hauled as you are passing the mark;
- and sheeting the sails in together.

Tactical Situations which Frequently Develop to Windward

A number of tactical situations often develop during a race and these should be used to gain an advantage.

1. *Lee-bow situation*
The following situation is a useful attacking manoeuvre to improve your tactical position and is commonly used in:

- the starting area
- approaching the windward mark

If used correctly, the effect can be quite dramatic on a boat on your weather quarter which you rather wish wasn't there! The 'lee-bow effect' is one legal way of getting rid of this boat (Plate 41).

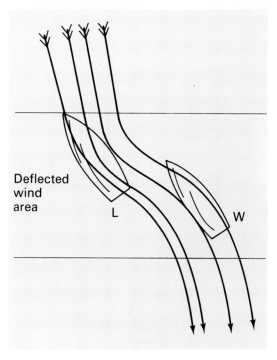

Fig. 34.
W in effect is sailing in a deflected wind area and will slowly drop astern and to leeward.

Plate 41. 39978 and 39966 are in a lee-bow situation. The deflected wind coming off the sail of 39978 is causing 39966 to slow down. The latter must consider tacking to clear her wind.

The way to achieve a good lee-bow effect in a two-boat situation on open water is as follows (Fig. 34):

- get as close as possible under the opposition's lee-bow;
- create a fairly hard mainsail leach;
- boom on or near the centre-line;
- balance the boat slightly to windward;
- pinch the boat slightly.

By doing the above you cause the maximum deflection of wind into the sail area of the boat on your weather quarter and

the other boat will be headed and slow down. Try it with a friend during a training session.

2. *Starting a windward leg*

No matter which position you are holding, be it first, second, or third, etc., you must *always stay between the opposition and the windward mark* during a windward leg (Plate 42 *see page 79*). If you do not, you are giving the opposition the opportunity to break through and get ahead of you. In your pre-race preparation you will have decided whether to go left or right up the windward leg, or to play the shifts up the middle. Often during a race, the pattern of the second, third and fourth windward legs may have been set by the leaders after the first beat, so

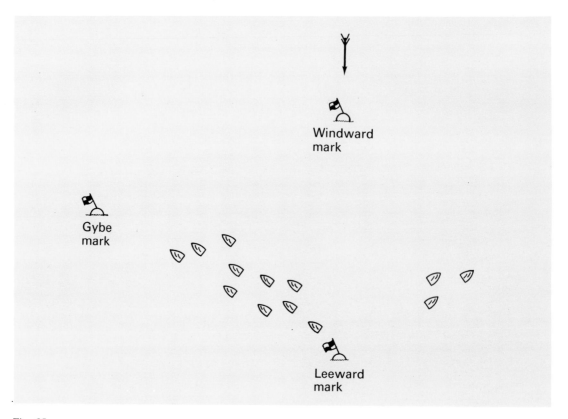

Fig. 35.
Always consolidate, unless you know something that the main group of boats is unaware of.

Fig. 36.
In this example of two boats racing: in position 1, the leading boat approaches the leeward mark. In position 2, with the leeward mark half-way between the leading boat and the second boat, the leading boat tacks. In position 3, as the second boat rounds the leeward mark, the leading boat is able to cover the second boat all the way up the beat.

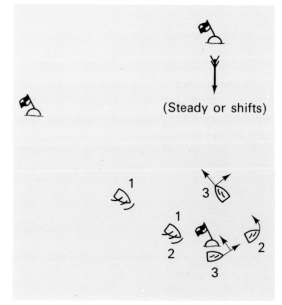

you know which is the favoured way to go.

Remember that in a fairly large fleet, it is advisable to stay between the main group and the windward mark. Never take a chance with the minority unless you are 100% certain that it is the correct way to go (Fig. 35).

Plate 42. The last beat – Laser 80963 sits tightly on the opposition all the way up the beat so as to safeguard his position.

just luffs up and carries on, you can tack and be on his weather bow. This is how you should progress all the way up the beat, not forgetting or ignoring what the rest of the fleet is doing, or letting the other boat take you the wrong way up the beat.

3. Shepherding the opposition from ahead
If you are ahead of your main opposition you can dictate which way you want them to go

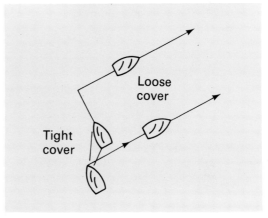

Fig. 37.
Make the opposition go the way you want them to go. It can work for the boat astern too!

As you round the leeward mark (Fig. 36) you should split the distance between yourself and the opposition, unless again you are certain that it is going to pay you to tack immediately and go to the lay-line, or stand on to the lay-line to gain the most advantage.

To clarify this: when the leeward mark is midway between yourself and the opposition you should take a covering tack up to windward. In this position, as the opposition rounds the mark, you are placed so that, if he tacks you are on his weather bow, or if he

up the windward leg by either tight or loose covering (Fig. 37). For example: if you want the opposition to go right up the beat, you would tight cover them on starboard tack and loose cover them on port tack. You employ the reverse tactics if you want them to go left.

This tactical manoeuvre can be very effective in getting the opposition to go the way you want them to go and keeping the fleet together as opposed to splitting it up. This manoeuvre can also be used to make a boat be on the wrong side of an expected wind bend or windshift, by being to leeward of you and outside the wind bend/shift whilst

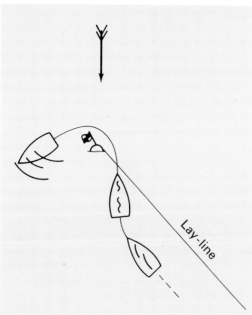

Fig. 38.
Here the boat luffs head to wind with her momentum carrying her around the buoy.

Plate 43. This Laser demonstrates how to 'shoot the mark'. Unable to lay it on starboard tack, as he approaches the buoy he luffs up head to wind and the speed of the boat takes him past the mark. This action saves having to put in two tacks which would result in the loss of a lot of ground.

you are being freed.

If the opposition do not toe the line and they split behind you, then all you can do is go the way which you think is correct, and sail as fast as possible so as to stay ahead.

4. *One boat approaching a windward mark: shooting the mark*

If you are approaching the mark slightly below the lay-line (Fig. 38), as opposed to making two tacks to round the mark, luff up, head to wind with both or one sail flapping, and allow the speed of the boat to take you round the buoy. This will save you quite a few boat lengths, if executed correctly (Plate 43).

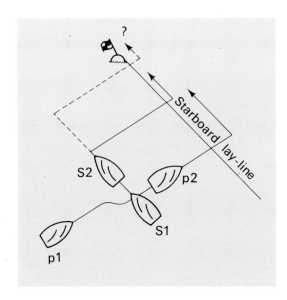

Fig. 39.

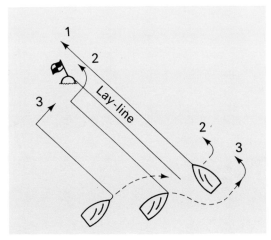

Fig. 40.

5. *Two boats approaching a windward mark*

Fig. 39 demonstrates a situation which is common when approaching the windward mark. The port tack boat has to bear away around the starboard boat's stern. If both boats now carry on, the next time the two boats meet, the boat on port tack stands a strong chance of rounding the windward mark first (marks to port). However, the starboard boat, having fulfilled Rules 35 and 41, should immediately tack and stay between the port boat and the windward mark so that she can still be ahead at the windward mark as shown in the diagram.

6. *Three boats approaching a windward mark*

Another situation which frequently develops is the three-boat situation, one on starboard and two on port, with the starboard boat on the starboard lay-line (Fig. 40).

The leeward port boat lying third could turn this situation to her tactical advantage by calling to the windward port boat under Rule 34 and 43–'Water for a starboard tack boat'. The windward port tack boat must tack and so must the leeward port tack boat, so that all three boats are approaching the windward mark on starboard with only the windward boat laying the mark. The middle boat can now sail the leeward boat up to and beyond the port lay-line and round the windward mark second, as opposed to third, if the manoeuvre is executed correctly.

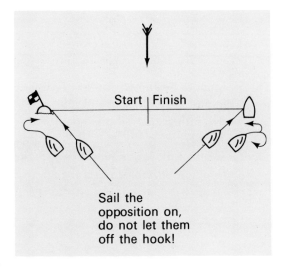

Fig. 41.

Tactics at Marks

1. *Starting/finishing line*

At the port end, on starboard tack on the lay-line, with a boat to leeward, sail that boat on to and beyond the lay-line so that you secure your position (Fig. 41 *see page 81*). Similarly at the starboard end on port tack, sail the opposition on to and beyond the lay-line.

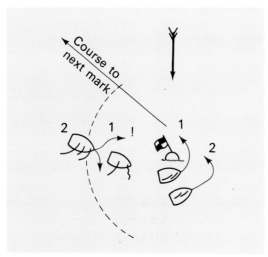

Fig. 42.
Consider defending your position by slowing down.

2. *Slow down!*

There is a lot to be gained and lost tactically at marks, and very often it will pay you to slow down rather than think about going faster (Fig. 42).

For example: if you have a boat close astern as you are approaching a mark; or if your tacking or gybing manoeuvre is restricted under Rule 41; or if you wish to be clear to tack or gybe without a boat close astern, it will pay you to slow down on arriving at the two boat lengths radius circle. This action will force the boat astern to pass

outside of you, as it is not allowed at this stage to barge in between you and the mark.

Another situation when it will pay you to

Fig. 43.
Gain the advantage by slowing down and making a better rounding of the mark.

slow down is on the outside of a 'raft' rounding a gybe or leeward mark (Fig. 43). Let the 'raft' go round. Having slowed down, you can now come around the mark

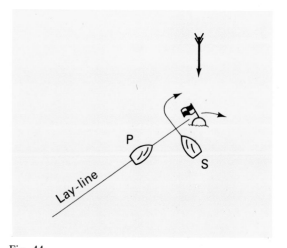

Fig. 44.
P should round the mark first, using Rules 35 and 41. The only defence for *S* would be to slow down.

making a correct rounding and you will be in a position to tack and go for clear wind.

3. Rounding the windward mark: port and starboard marks to starboard

In this case, theoretically, with the port boat on the lay-line, the starboard boat is in the lead, but if executed properly the port boat will round the mark first (Fig. 44). The starboard boat is in the right under Rule 36 but not under Rule 41, so the port boat should round the mark first.

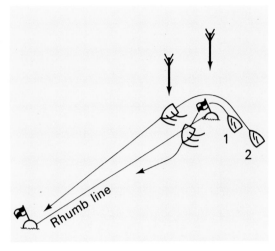

Fig. 45.
Boat 2 gains the advantage by delaying the spinnaker hoist and getting on top of boat 1.

Plate 44 *below*. 470–K397 and 420–K38285 makes a good approach to effect a good rounding of the leeward mark. 28744's entry appears to be too narrow and as a result the exit may be too wide.

4. *Rounding the windward mark close astern*

Another tactical gain around the windward mark (Fig. 45 *see page 83*), is when sailing close astern of another boat. Should he bear away straight for the next mark, this allows you to attack his weather quarter. Also while the opposition is sorting out the spinnaker, if

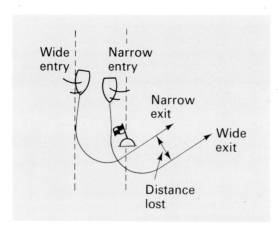

Fig. 46.
Do not gybe at the mark as this will result in a poor rounding. Gybe earlier to make a good rounding.

you are sailing close astern, you can sail over the top of him. Always look out for such opportunities as soon as you round the windward mark and so gain the advantage.

5. *Rounding the leeward mark*

Here too a tactical advantage can be gained. Many sailors approach the leeward mark-especially at the end of the dead run-at far too narrow an angle and subsequently make a bad rounding of the mark with a wide-angle exit (Fig. 46), (Plate 44 *see page 83*).

If you are on the outside of a situation like this it will pay you to slow down, make a wide entry into the mark with a good rounding and narrow exit, passing the mark close hauled. By doing this you will be well

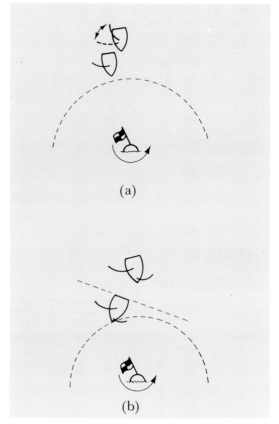

Fig. 47.
(a) Slow down as the overtaking boat to gain the overlap at the right moment.
(b) Bear away boldly to break an overlap at the correct time.

up on the weather quarter of a boat making a poor rounding and in a position to tack off into clear wind, if that is what you require to do. You will also be in clear wind if you do not wish to tack.

6. *Overlap at marks*

The leeward mark is also the place to be thinking about either gaining or breaking an overlap. This also applies at the gybe mark. You can proceed all the way down a run or reach near the opposition.' The important thing is to round the mark with the tactical advantage. This will decide which boat will have the overlap at the mark and be ahead.

Let us look at a typical example of two boats close to each other approaching the leeward mark at the end of the running leg. The boats are at this stage clear ahead and clear astern. As you make your final approach to the leeward mark two boat lengths radius circle, the boat clear astern should consider manoeuvring into a positon dead astern so as to blanket the boat ahead and, if closing too fast, slow down so that as the leading boat approaches the two boat lengths circle, you are in a position to gain an overlap on his weather quarter at the correct time (Fig. 47 (a)).

As the boat clear ahead during this build-up, your only defence is to boldly bear away as you enter the circle (Fig. 47 (b)) so as to break the overlap, and tell the boat astern 'No water'. Do not forget that as you round a mark, if there is a collision, the onus of proof in the protest room is on the person calling 'Water' or 'No water', as to whether the overlap was or was not established in the proper time.

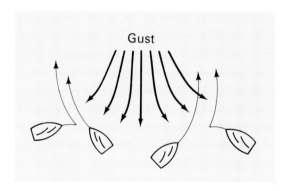

Fig. 48.
Be prepared to use a gust as a freeing or heading shift to your advantage.

Tactics when Racing in Gusts and Squalls

GUSTS

When racing in gusty conditions, your tactics to windward must take into consideration the gusts themselves and what you should do (Fig. 48).

As a gust approaches, you must look at it as a complete entity in relation to your boat. If the gust is fine on the weather bow or almost dead ahead, be prepared to be headed, and tack. If the gust is broad on the beam, be ready to be freed on that tack around the edge of the gust.

SQUALLS

When racing during squally conditions, you must consider that ahead of a squall—which you may see approaching the racing area to windward—there will be a backing wind and also an increasing wind so you need to be on port tack as it approaches (Fig. 49 *see page 86*). As the squall comes overhead and passes, the wind underneath and behind the squall will be a veering and decreasing wind and you should now be on starboard tack being freed. This theory only applies in the Northern hemisphere, and it is the opposite Down Under!

When racing under high pressure and cumulus clouds, there is less wind slightly ahead and under the track of the clouds where the air is rising, and there is more wind to be found under the clear blue sky areas. Look for these and use them, making sure you are on the freeing tack, allowing for tide and surface current if applicable.

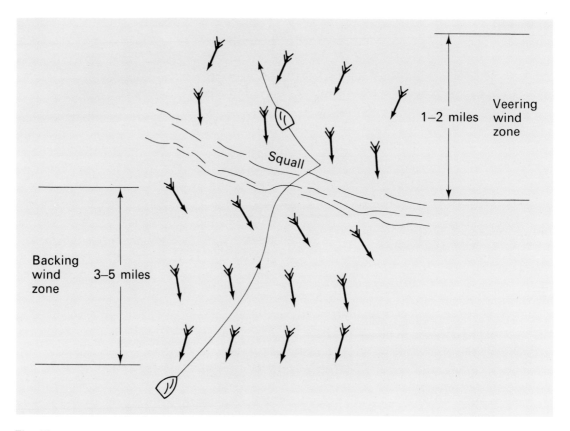

Fig. 49.
In squally conditions, look for the port lift ahead of the
squall, and the starboard behind it.

6
Compass Work

The theory of compass work and windshift tracking is often talked about, but only a few put it into practice!

A readable compass, correctly sited in the boat, is absolutely essential when racing in relatively large fleets on the open sea.
However it is not essential when sailing in enclosed waters, for reasons which will become obvious as we look at the subject.

Once you have acquired a good compass, have it sited in the middle of the boat where it can be clearly seen by the helmsman and because of weight considerations, place it as low down as possible. Naturally this varies from class to class. The advantage of having the compass placed centrally in the boat and also forward in the mast area, is that the angle of vision for the helmsman, from the waves approaching the bow to the tell-tales to the compass, is as narrow as possible (Fig. 50). Also ideally, it should be a vertically facing one so that it can be clearly seen (Fig. 51).

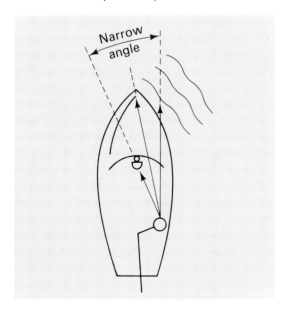

Fig. 50.
Keep the angle of vision as narrow as possible.

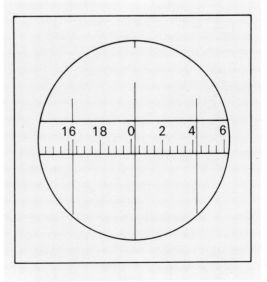

Fig. 51.
Use a vertical facing compass with clear graduation.

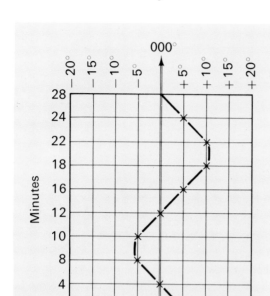

Fig. 52.
At start time the freeing tack is the starboard tack.

Uses of a Compass in Racing

Apart from providing a psychological boost, the compass must be used for the following:

- windshift tracking
- starting line
- windshifts
- wind bends
- reaching legs
- rounding the leeward mark
- sighting a newly laid windward mark.

WINDSHIFT TRACKING

Prior to the start, it is important to track the wind to see what it is doing, establish a pattern and relate your tracking pattern to the weather forecast.

You can detect whether or not the wind is steadily veering or backing in accordance with the forecast, or whether it is an oscillating wind around a mean wind direction. You should take wind readings every two–four minutes and mark the readings on your tracking card so that you know what the wind may be expected to do at the start time (Fig. 52). This will help you to decide which end of the line to be and which tack is the freeing tack off the line, which is very important.

STARTING LINES

While preparing for the race, give yourself enough time to select the correct end (fixed line)—allowing for distance, wind strength and time—and you must check the starting line for bias and see which end is nearer to the wind.

Once you are at the correct end of the line you must check to see if the wind is right of its mean direction, or if it is going right. If it is, you need to be on starboard tack and if the opposite, on port tack off the line—refer to your windshift tracking chart (see Appendix IV).

WINDSHIFTS

Once on a windward leg, the compass is now used to detect wind shifts (Fig. 53 (a)), whether or not you are being lifted or headed on either tack. When racing in a land-locked area (Fig. 53 (b)), a compass is not essential as you can immediately see by relating your jib luff—or in the cast of singlehangers, your main luff—against the shoreline to see whether or not you are being lifted or headed.

When sailing in shifty conditions as on a

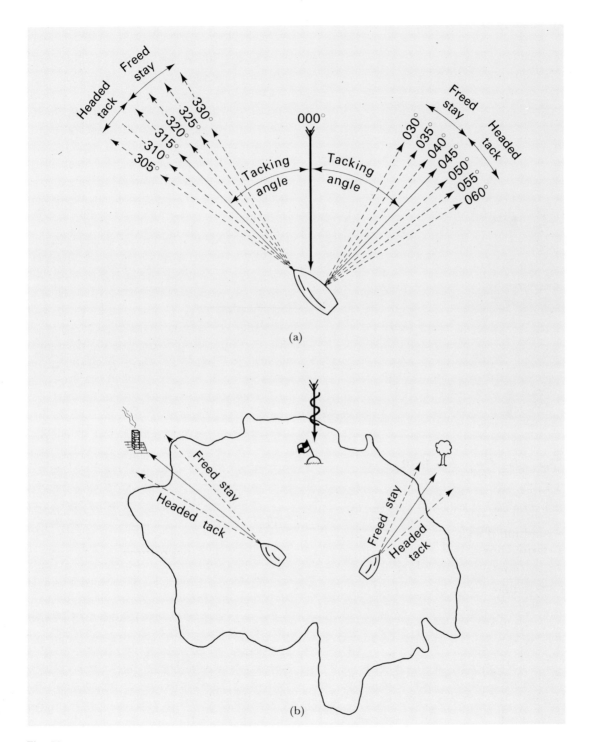

Fig. 53.
(a) In a non land-locked venue, use a compass to gain advantage to windward.

(b) Use landmarks in a land-locked venue, if there is no compass.

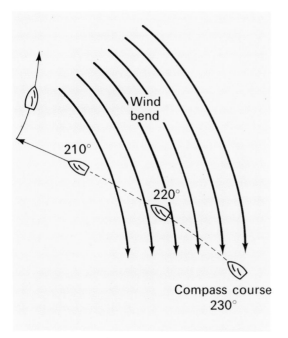

Fig. 54.
This example shows the boat being slowly headed on
the long starboard tack as it sails into the wind bend.

lake, reservoir, river estuary or up to a high
windward shore, always remember that as
you are being lifted on a tack, stay on it, if
you are being headed, then tack.

WIND BENDS

As already mentioned in Chapter 1 under
'geographical preparations', there could well
be a built-in wind bend over the race area
with the wind in a particular direction and
you must use the compass to detect this prior
to the start time.

The only way to do this is by sailing the
windward leg on one tack, and if you have
time do both, to confirm whether or not a
bend exists. As you go to windward, you
must observe the compass as you do either
the long port or the starboard tack, and

watch whether or not you are being steadily
lifted or headed as you go along (Fig. 54).

Once you have established that the bend
exists, you then plan your start to ensure
that you are one of the first, if not *the* first to
get into and take advantage of it.

REACHING LEGS

In the case of a reaching leg, the compass
only comes into use if the gybe mark is
unsighted due to mist and/or drizzle, so that
you can steer a course for the mark. Also, by
knowing the distance between the windward
mark, the gybe mark and leeward mark, and
by guessing your average boat speed and
allowing for the tide (if any), you can work
out how long it will take you to get to each
mark, so that you can concentrate on
looking for it.

The formula to use is:

$$\frac{D}{S \times T} \times \frac{60}{1}$$

D = Distance   S = Speed   T = Time

ROUNDING THE LEEWARD MARK

Having rounded the leeward mark, the
correct use of a compass when racing on the
open sea is essential, whereas on a land-
locked venue, transits may be used if you do
not have a compass.

As soon as you have settled down, having
completed your rounding of the mark, it is
important to check your compass-reading
immediately and assess whether or not you
are being headed or freed from the course
you were on the last time you were in the
leeward mark area (Fig. 55).

If you are being headed you must assess
the following straight away:

- whether to tack;
- is the wind starting to veer in accordance with the weather forecast, the cloud formation and/or frontal system?

If the wind is starting to veer, you may wish to carry on on this header in order to be inside this new wind shift. If this is not the case and the wind is expected to stay in the same direction, you should tack straight away on to the freeing tack if in a strategic position to do so.

If you find yourself on a lift having gone round the mark, you should likewise assess whether you should carry on, or tack to get inside a new wind direction which is developing.

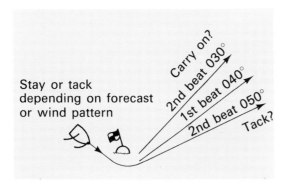

Fig. 55.

SIGHTING A NEWLY LAID WINDWARD MARK

At most major events a change of wind direction means a change of the course and therefore a new windward mark (Fig. 56).

As you round the leeward mark, if the

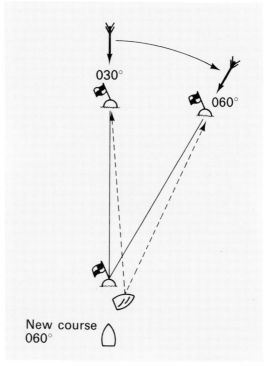

Fig. 56.
Use a compass to sight a new mark.

race committee is indicating a new windward leg, you must identify the new windward mark from the course indicated on the committee boat, as the old windward mark may still be down and you may end up heading for the wrong windward mark from the leeward mark. Using your compass, make sure you sight the new windward mark and establish its position in relation to the old one.

7
Mark Rounding

The Finer Points of Boat Handling

Many sailors have problems during a rounding manoeuvre, mostly because of poor boat handling ability (Plate 45). In the main, the problems are:

- not being able to bear away around the windward mark;
- broaching and/or capsizing, having just rounded the windward mark;

- poor spinnaker gybes, resulting in twisted spinnakers (Plate 46 *on following pages*);
- broaching and/or capsizing around the leeward mark (Plate 47 *see page 95*).

Most of the above problems arise during medium to strong winds, but some,

Plate 45. A good example of how not to round the windward mark. The board position is fine (half up) but the mainsheet needs easing out, the boat trim is too far forward and the weight should be further aft and further out.

Plate 46 (a). No control of the spinnaker by the
helmswoman.

Plate 46 (b). Twisted spinnaker, either incorrectly packed or not lowered correctly the last time.

Plate 46 (c) *above*. Poor gybe–no control of boat balance or spinnaker.

especially poor spinnaker gybes resulting in a twisted spinnaker, occur in the lighter wind range too. The next section looks at the problems of boat handling around marks in more detail, and tries to eliminate the mistakes being made.

Rounding the Windward Mark– Doublehanders

Often in medium to strong winds, boats sail round the windward mark balanced to leeward, with the rudder blades making that familiar gurgling sound. This means that the sails are not being used to turn the boat away from the wind, and as a result they broach and maybe capsize.

If you round the windward mark in medium to strong winds in a doublehanded boat using the jib and mainsail and

Plate 47. Leeward broach capsize due to centreboard being too far down.

Plate 48. A good example of how to use body-weight to assist the boat to bear away with the least amount of tiller movement, and reducing the risk of broaching by raising the lee-bow off the water.

bodyweight for balance, this stalling and broaching will not happen. You must go around the weather mark with the least amount of rudder movement by getting the boat in balance to steer itself (Plate 48).

First of all, the boat balance must be kept upright and slightly to windward. As you bear away initially, the jib is kept in and eased more slowly than the mainsail. At the same time, the combined weight of the helmsman and crew must come aft along the gunwale, to enable the lee-bow to lift off the water so that the bow will want to go off to leeward.

The extent that the lee-bow lifts off the water depends on the type of boat you sail. It is very effective in boats with deep 'V'

sections forward of the mast and with large genoas and also, in boats with large mainsails and small jibs.

By combining the above points, you will round the weather mark in balance with the least amount of rudder and pressure. It will also pay to raise the board a little before you bear away.

Rounding the Windward Mark– Singlehanders

Basically the same applies to singlehanders as it does to doublehanders, except that it is very important to make your board adjustment before you round the mark and, in the case of the Laser and Topper, make the necessary clew and kicking strap adjustments prior to the rounding—with the mainsail in and the boat balanced slightly to windward. Do not bring the board up too much as you may capsize to windward having borne away.

Rounding the Gybe Mark–Doublehanders

The main problem here is the spinnaker handling and carrying out a controlled gybe. Keeping in mind what has already been said about boat handling at the gybe mark, let us look at the spinnaker control sequence itself (Plate 49 *see this and following page*).

The most common spinnaker pole system is the single double-ended pole, with the up- and down-haul system in the centre of the pole.

SPINNAKER CONTROL SEQUENCE

1. As the boat goes into the gybe, the **crew** must start to square the spinnaker round as the **helmsman** bears away. This brings the boat to the dead run position.

2. The **helmsman** stands up and takes both guy and sheet, holding the tiller between his knees.

3. The **crew:**

- releases the guy out of the reaching hook;
- releases the pole off the mast, passing the end forward of the mast;
- comes aft in the boat;
- gybes the mainsail, and in moving the weight back, assists in raising the bow out of the water.

4. The **helmsman** assists the mainsail gybe by bearing away further, and at the same time, keeps the spinnaker full.

Plate 49 (a). The spinnaker pole is off the mast.

Plate 49 (b). Crew has the end of the pole in front of him on completion of the gybe, to put straight onto the new guy.

Plate 50 *above*. Singlehanded heavy weather gybing. The helm must be quicker in crossing the boat and centralizing the tiller to avoid broaching to leeward.

5. On completion of the gybe, the **crew** goes forward and:

- grabs the end of the pole which is hanging in front of him;
- puts the new guy in;
- releases the old guy/new sheet;
- puts the pole on to the mast;
- then trims the guy in the reaching hook and takes the sheet.

6. The **helmsman** can now trim the jib and then go back to controlling the mainsail. (The jib could be trimmed by the **crew** prior to the gybe, if preferred.)

The same basic sequence applies to a single-ended pole system.

The aim of flicking the pole off the mast

Plate 49 (c). *opposite*. The spinnaker is kept full during the gybing manoeuvre by the helmsman.

prior to the gybe, is to prevent the crew fiddling around the front of the mast trying to get the pole off, *after* the gybe. This is the last place you want the crew's weight to be in medium to strong winds—with body-weight forward in the boat. This would cause the boat to nose dive and create the 'death roll', burying the lee-bow and capsizing the boat to leeward. This system is good when gybing from broad reach to broad reach, or run to run. It is not so critical to keep the spinnaker full when gybing from a close reach to a close reach or when defending your wind in a breeze.

Rounding the Gybe Mark– Singlehanders

In a singlehander, as you bear away into the gybe, you must ease the mainsail with the boat trimmed fairly well aft (Plate 50). At the same time as bearing away, look for the leach starting to move and as it starts, go across the boat quickly to prevent the outboard end of the boom hitting the water on completion of the gybe.

Also, on completion of the gybe, be prepared to pull the mainsail in to prevent the boat possibly capsizing to windward. You have to be quick in a breeze, which brings us back to flexibility in the body, speed of reaction and fitness!

Rounding the Leeward Mark– Doublehanders

The main problems which arise with doublehanders usually are:

- misjudging the speed of approach, and taking the spinnaker down too late or too

Plate 51 *below*. Spinnaker taken down too late for the rounding. It is important to judge the speed of approach more accurately.

early (Plate 51);
- taking the spinnaker (non-shute boats) down incorrectly—so the next time it goes up, it is twisted;
- altering boat tuning controls too late;
- balancing the boat to leeward, resulting in broaching.

The speed of approach to the leeward mark must be understood, so that you are ready to round the leeward mark with the spinnaker stowed, and the cunningham hole, kicking strap, clew outhaul and centre-board adjustments all made, so that the boat is set up correctly for the next windward leg.

The centreboard can be adjusted after rounding in stronger winds so as to reduce the risk of broaching during the rounding. In non-shute boats, the spinnaker must be taken down to windward—having got rid of

Plate 52. Adjustments to the cunningham hole are made before rounding the leeward mark. In a strong breeze, adjustment to board, kicker and clew outhaul should be made after the rounding.

the pole—the guy should be pulled until the tack of the spinnaker is in hand, then the helmsman releases the halliard and the spinnaker is pulled down by the luff, and the rest on top. This will guarantee that the spinnaker will not go up twisted the next time.

Another point which is sometimes forgotten is the tightening up of the spinnaker sheets, either by the helmsman or the crew, so as to prevent them trailing astern.

Rounding the Leeward Mark– Singlehanders

When rounding the leeward mark in a singlehanded boat the following should be observed:

- in the lighter wind range, adjustments to the daggerboard, cunningham hole, kicking strap and clew outhaul should be made *prior* to the rounding;
- in medium to strong winds, apart from the cunningham hole, these adjustments should be done *after* the rounding (Plate 52).

Having rounded the leeward mark correctly, with the boat in balance—slightly pinched and balanced to windward in the case of a Laser and Topper—adjustments can be made to the kicking strap, clew and daggerboard. The tiller extension can be held between thumb and forefinger during these adjustments, or trapped under your backside!

By making these adjustments on completion of the rounding, you reduce the risk of broaching and/or capsizing and in any case, it is essential that they are done on completion of the rounding. It is important to get the daggerboard down after the rounding as this will reduce the risk of broaching and capsizing prior to the rounding.

8
Crewing

Crewing is an art and a skill, which like every other skill comes only with practice and experience. It requires fitness, agility and intelligence.

A good crew is worth his or her weight in gold and is as important as the helmsman. The crew is the lookout, the provider of constant information and the mobile ballast!

It is essential that the helmsman and crew are compatible. They must be able to get along well inside and outside the boat and they must be able to communicate. If they spend most of their time in the racing area not communicating, they have not only a personal problem but a major tactical disadvantage.

While racing, the helmsman must be allowed to concentrate on making the boat go as fast as possible, while the rest of the burden falls on the crew's shoulders. Crew and helmsman must know exactly which are their respective tasks, on all points of sailing and in all wind strengths. Only a lot of hard training and time spent on the water together, will produce the high standard necessary to win races at the top level of competition's.

In the dinghy world, the crew needs to be very agile, sharp and have very quick reflexes; speed of reaction must be good. In addition, all movement must be very sensitive to the needs of the boat, particularly in the light to medium wind range. Many crews are far too aggressive with the boat and sails in light conditions when sensitivity and lightness of touch are so important.

As well as relating to the helmsman in a race, the crew must also concentrate on:

• boat balance
• boat trim
• boat handling (roll tacking, gybing, spinnaker work)
• sail trim
• tactics
• racing rules
• centreboard position

The crew's concentration on these points must be constant, whatever the point of sailing, whatever the conditions, and whatever the position of the boat in the fleet.

Common Crewing Faults

The following are the most common faults of trapezing and non-trapezing crews:

1. Lack of fitness.

2. Slow reactions
3. Facing forward in both non-hanging out and trapezing conditions.
4. Facing forward while tacking (depending on layout of jib sheets).
5. Not communicating with the helmsman on what is happening outside the boat.
6. Trapezing crews—flat-footed on the gunwhale with legs too far apart. Also, not using forward hand to support the head (preventing neck-ache), when on a long tack.
7. Clothing—not streamlined enough offering too much wind resistance, bulky lifejackets, and general lack of suitability of clothing.

Up to 50% of your body heat can be lost through the head, so no matter how many wet suits or layers you are wearing, unless you are also wearing some sort of head-gear, you are losing a very large amount of body heat and will inevitably feel cold.

Some sailors wear clothing underneath their wet suits thereby defeating the object of the wet suit. The correct clothing for the conditions of the day is of paramount importance. If you get cold you will lose your concentration, and therefore the race!

Good crews take time to mature and get to their peak of perfection and efficiency. If as a helmsman you have been lucky enough to find a good crew, treasure and look after him or her! If you haven't found the perfect crew, find a willing body and train him or her with lots of practice and patience!

9
Racing Rules

The subject of the racing rules is a book on its own and I do not propose to go deeply into the subject. There are some very good books already available on the subject. However, I feel that it is important to remember the following:

1. The Racing Rules are both your attacking and defending weapon in the sport and you should have a thorough working knowledge of *Parts I and IV*. There can be nothing worse than doing well in a regatta, championship or race, only to be disqualified because your knowledge of the rules is inadequate.
2. Generally speaking, the standard of knowledge of the rules is poor in the UK. One of the reasons for this is that at Club level, after an incident afloat, most sailors do not discuss points of the race—they are in a rush to get away. The result of this is that when the situation develops again, they are none the wiser.
3. If the standard is poor at Club level, it continues to spread up to the Regional, National and International levels. Clubs should put more effort into running protest meetings and so help to raise the standard in the Club. Next time you are

involved in an incident, put your flag B up and learn by your mistakes!
4. There is nothing nasty about protests; they are part of racing and people's attitudes should change towards this aspect of the sport to improve knowledge of the rules and protest procedures.

The Racing Rules can be broken down into the following parts:

PART I

Definitions
There are seventeen definitions altogether and it is important to know them.

PART II

Management of Races [Rules 1–14]
A good working knowledge of these rules is required to appreciate fully what will happen both ashore and afloat, under the direction of the Race Committee or Jury.

PART III

General Requirements [Rules 18–28]
This section covers the responsibility of an owner to qualify his or her boat for a race.

PART IV

Right of Way Rules [Rules 31–46]
A thorough knowledge is required here, as
these are the rules which apply when racing
(except for yachts racing at night).

PART V

*Other Sailing Rules–Obligations of
Helmsman and Crew in Handling a Yacht*
[Rules 50–66]
This section covers numerous obligations
from ranking as a starter to increasing
stability.

PART VI

Protests, Disqualifications and Appeals
[Rules 68–78]
A thorough working knowledge of this
section is required. Many sailors have little
or no experience of protest precedures
(because they do not bother at Club level!).
They may have been in the right on the
water but they lose in the protest room
because they do not know what to say or
when to say it and have no confidence in
protest procedures, or the rules. Make it
your business to be familiar with these rules!

   Part IV of the Racing Rules, [Rules
31–46], the Right of Way Rules, are outlined
and clarified below. These rules *always* apply
whilst racing.The rules in this part fall into
three sections. These are as follows:

Section A: Obligations and Penalties

Key

Wrong

Right

Wind

RULE 31: DISQUALIFICATION

This rule says that you can be disqualified
for infringing any of the rules in *Part IV*
whilst racing or for infringing any of the
sailing instructions, whether you are racing
or not.

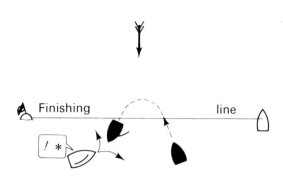

Black, having cleared the finishing line, may still be
disqualified for hindering *White* which is still racing
(31.2). This is also an occasion where port has right of
way over starboard.

RULE 32: AVOIDING COLLISIONS

Even if you have got the right of way, this
does not give you the right to sail straight
through the opposition. You may be
disqualified if you involve yourself in a
collision which results in serious damage.

You may be right under Rule 36 as the starboard tack yacht, but not under Rule 32 where you may be disqualified if serious damage occurs. Also look out for the insurance man!

RULE 33: RULE INFRINGEMENT

If you are aware that you have infringed a rule or sailing instruction, you must retire promptly, or exonerate yourself by accepting an alternative penalty if prescribed in the Sailing Instructions.

Rule 33 also says that if there is contact between boats during a race, both shall be disqualified unless one or the other retires, exonerates himself or protests. If the incident was caused by the Race Committee, it may waive the infringement or disqualification, when it is satisfied that contact was minor and unavoidable.

Do not forget that under this rule a third boat witnessing the incident will have both boats disqualified if neither does anything about it. So if you are in an incident and are in the right, you must protest or you may be disqualified yourself!

RULE 34: HAILING

You must hail to clarify a developing situation that may be unforeseen by the opposition, even if you are in the right, for example, luffing before starting, tacking, establishing or terminating an overlap, or taking someone the wrong side of the mark. The only time a hail is not required is when luffing after starting, under Rule 38.

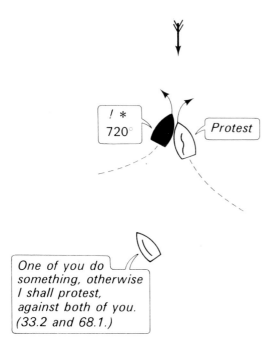

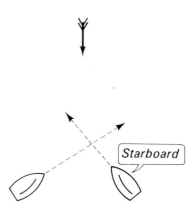

A hail, although not always necessary, helps to clarify a situation. Typical examples of this are shown here.

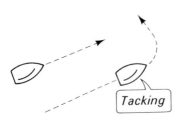

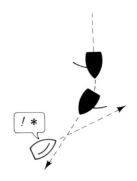

Section B: Principal Right of Way Rules and their Limitations

These rules apply except when over-ridden by a rule in section C.

RULE 35: LIMITATIONS ON ALTERING COURSE

This rule states quite clearly that, if you have got the right of way, you are not allowed to alter course so as to prevent the other boat from trying to keep clear, or to obstruct her while she is keeping clear.

The only exception to this is when luffing after starting; assuming a proper course to start; or when rounding a mark. When regaining rights – having been a premature starter – you must give a boat starting correctly, ample room and opportunity to keep clear.

RULE 36: OPPOSITE TACKS—BASIC RULE

This rule is straightforward and causes relatively little bother whilst on the course. It states initially that; a port tack yacht shall keep clear of a starboard tack yacht. There are, however, a few occasions when a port tack yacht has right of way over a starboard tack yacht and you should know them!

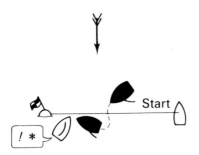

Two more situations when the starboard tack boat is in the wrong: this time under Rule 35.

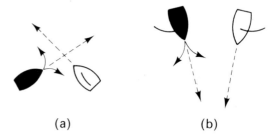

(a)   (b)

(a) *Black* must keep clear by either luffing, tacking or bearing away.
(b) Here *Black* must keep clear by bearing away, gybing or luffing around the stern of *White*.

RULE 37: SAME TACK—BASIC RULE

This rule is broken down into three part:

1. When overlapped, a windward yacht shall keep clear of a leeward yacht.
2. When not overlapped, a yacht clear astern shall keep clear of a yacht clear ahead.
3. This is transitional. If you establish an overlap to leeward from clear astern, you must give the windward yacht ample room and opportunity to keep clear. In other words, if you establish this overlap and the windward boat luffs to keep clear and her leeward quarter touches your weather bow, you have not given her enough room to keep clear. You must also give her time to keep clear before insisting on your rights as the leeward boat.

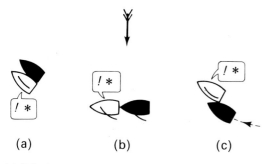

(a)   (b)   (c)

(a) Windward. Leeward. (37.1).

(b) Clear ahead. Clear astern. (32.2).

(c) Having established an overlap to leeward, *Black* must give *White* ample room and opportunity to keep clear. (37.3).

RULE 38: SAME TACK—LUFFING AND SAILING
ABOVE A PROPER COURSE AFTER STARTING

Rule 38 is broken down into six parts and can be summed up as follows:

Having cleared the starting line after the starting signal, a yacht either clear ahead or overlapped to leeward may luff as she pleases, subject to the proper course limitations of this rule.

The proper course limitations of the rule are: that a leeward yacht shall not sail above her proper course while an overlap exists, if at any time during the overlap the helmsman of the windward boat is abreast or forward of the mast-abeam position.

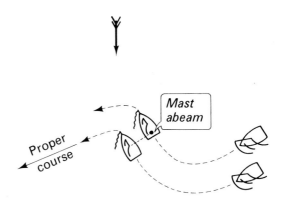

(a) A leeward yacht may luff as she pleases up to and including head-to-wind unless the mast abeam position is reached beforehand when the leeward boat must assume her proper course for the next mark (38.1 and 38.2).

An overlap only exists between two boats when they are clearly within two boat lengths of the longer boat. If one or both boats either tack or gybe a new overlap is established at that time.

(b) Here an overlap exists under Rule 38.3.

(c) A new overlap exists the moment the windward boat completes her tack (38.3).

If there is any doubt, hail to stop or prevent a luff. A leeward yacht may luff unless the helmsman of the windward yacht hails 'Mast abeam', or words to that effect! Having received such a hail, the leeward yacht must assume her proper course for the next mark, and if she considers it improper, her only remedy is to protest.

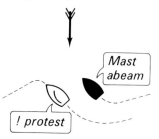

(d) An improper call, *White* must bear away and protest (38.4).

With regard to preventing a luff as the windward boat, you can only do this if you are unable to respond due to a third boat to windward or an obstruction.

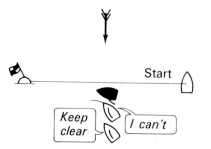

(e) The middle boat curtails the luff under Rule 38.5. The leeward boat protest *White* and *Black*.

If you wish to luff two or more yachts you must have luffing rights over all boats affected by your luff.

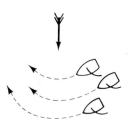

(f) The leeward boat has luffing rights on both boats, although the middle boat does not on the windward boat. They must both respond under Rule 38.6.

RULE 39: SAME TACK—SAILING BELOW A
PROPER COURSE AFTER STARTING

When on a free leg of the course, you are not allowed to sail below your proper course for the mark to prevent a boat passing to leeward when the boats are within three boat lengths of each other. Do not forget that this also applies when you have a boat dead astern trying to establish an overlap to leeward, as at a gybemark for example.

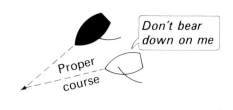

(a) The only rule in the book where three boat lengths are mentioned, and on a free leg of the course.

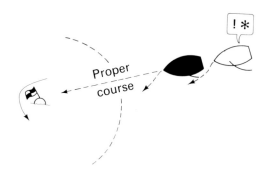

(b) The same applies here with a boat clear ahead, she must not bear away to cut off the boat astern.

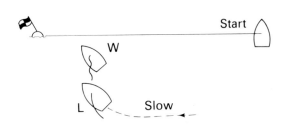

(b) Windward (*W*) does not have to do anything until an overlap is established, then she must be given ample room and opportunity to keep clear.

RULE 40: SAME TACK—LUFFING BEFORE
STARTING

Rule 40 states quite clearly that any luff which is carried out before the starting signal, shall be carried out slowly and that you must give the boat being luffed ample room and opportunity to keep clear. If the windward boat chooses to luff to keep clear and her leeward quarter touches your windward bow, then you have not given the windward boat ample room to keep clear.

You can, if you have luffing rights, luff up to and including head-to-wind before and after the starting signal. Without luffing rights you can only luff up to and including a close hauled course.

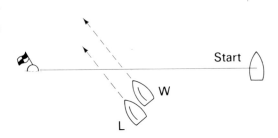

(c) *L* can only sail up to and including a close hauled course when abaft mast abeam.

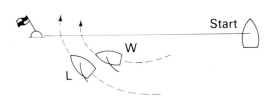

(a) Leeward (*L*) can luff up to and including-head-to wind slowly both before and after the starting signal.

Hailing to stop or prevent a luff, curtailing a luff, and luffing two or more yachts under Rule 38 also applies.

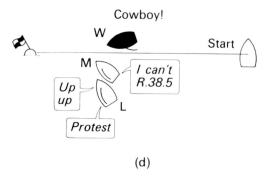

(d)

(d) Here *L* can protest the middle boat (*M*), who in turn will protest *W* who will be disqualified unless a 720° turn applies and is carried out.

RULE 41: CHANGING TACKS—TACKING AND GYBING

A yacht which is either tacking or gybing shall keep clear of a yacht on a tack.

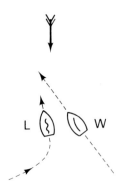

(a) *L* tacking, must keep clear of *W*.

When you decide either to tack or to gybe, you must do so far enough away from another boat to fulfil the requirements of this rule. You cannot tack or gybe close to another boat so that she has to take avoiding action before the tack or gybe has been completed. It will also pay you to hail under Rule 34 to clarify a situation when tacking or gybing in close proximity to another boat.

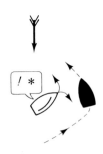

(b) *Black* tacks too close to *White* (41.2 and 41.3).

Do not forget that the onus of proof is on the tacking or gybing boat if you end up in front of a protest committee. When two boats are tacking or gybing simultaneously and close to each other, should there be a collision, remember that if you are on the right, you are right.

(c) If yachts are tacking simultaneously and a collision occurs remember, if you are on the right, you are right. Look out for the fundamental rule of fair sailing!

Section C: Rules which Apply at Marks and Obstructions

RULE 42: ROUNDING OR PASSING MARKS AND OBSTRUCTIONS

This is the longest and to some people the most complicated rule in the book. Broken down into four parts, it is relatively easy.

42.1. Room at marks and obstructions when overlapped

When yachts either on the same tack or—after starting and clearing the starting line—on opposite tacks, are about to round or pass a mark on the same required side or an obstruction on the same side, the following should be observed:

(a) An outside yacht shall give each yacht overlapping her on the inside, enough room to round or pass the mark or obstruction. Enough room must be allowed for an overlapping yacht to tack or gybe when either is an integral part of the rounding or passing manoeuvre.

(a) *L* must give *W* room to round the mark inside (42.1 (a)).

This applies except when the following occur: 42.1(c)—tacking to round the mark obstruction within two boat lengths, 42.1(d)—luffing a boat the wrong side of a mark and 42.4(a)—at a starting mark surrounded by navigable water.

(b) If you are the inside boat overlapping without luffing rights—whether on the same or opposite tacks—and have to gybe in order to assume your proper course for the next mark, you must do it at the first reasonable opportunity.

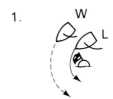

(b) 1. *W* must gybe and assume a proper course at the first reasonable opportunity (42.1 (b)).

2. *L* can carry on taking *W* away from the proper course to the next mark (42.1 b).

(c) If two boats are approaching the windward mark or obstruction on opposite tacks and one has to tack, Rule 42.1. will not apply and they are subject instead to Rules 36 and 41.

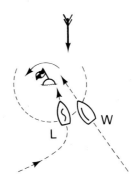

(c) Rule 42 does not apply here. It is as if the mark was taken away. *L* must observe Rules 36 and 41. She then uses Rules 37.1 and 38 to round the mark.

(d) An outside leeward yacht with luffing rights may take an inside yacht to windward of a mark provided that she hails to that effect and begins to luff before she is within two of her overall lengths of the mark and provided that she also passes to windward of it.

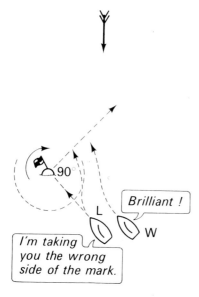

(d) If *W* slows and ducks to leeward of *L*, *L* does not have to carry on to windward, but may also go for the inside berth at the mark.

42.2. *Clear astern and clear ahead in the vicinity of marks and obstructions*

When yachts are about to round or pass a mark, other than a starting mark surrounded by navigable water on the required side, or an obstruction on the same side, the following should be observed:

(a) A yacht clear astern shall keep clear in anticipation of and during the rounding or passing manoeuvre when the yacht clear ahead remains on the same tack or gybes.

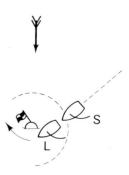

(a) Boat (*S*), must keep clear of L during the rounding and passing manoeuvre.

(b) A yacht which tacks to round a mark is subject to Rule 41. But a yacht clear astern cannot luff above a close hauled course so to prevent a yacht clear ahead tacking.

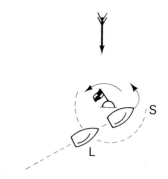

(b) *S* must not infringe Rule 41. During the rounding manoeuvre, *L* must not luff above close hauled to prevent S from tacking.

42.3 *Limitations on establishing and maintaining an overlap in the vicinity of marks and obstructions*

(a) A yacht clear astern may establish an inside overlap and be entitled to room only when the yacht clear ahead:

- is able to give the required room;
- is outside two lengths radius of the

mark, except if one yacht tacks inside this two length radius, or when an obstruction is a continuous one.

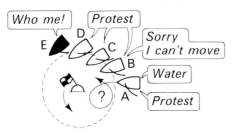

(a) *A* is not entitled to force a passage. She must either slow down or gybe round out of this situation. Her only remedy is to protest *B* who in turn protests *C* who protests *D,* and *D* protests *E. E* is diaqualified for not giving room, not *B.*

(b) A yacht clear ahead does not have to do anything until an overlap is established.

(c) If an overlap is established in proper time, it shall be continued even though it may subsequently be broken within two boat lengths of the mark.

(d) If you claim an inside overlap, the onus

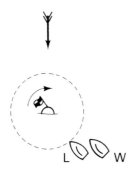

(b) *W* has established her overlap in proper time and is entitled to room at the mark. If the overlap is thereafter broken, *W* is still entitled to room should it be required.

of proof that you did it correctly, is on you.

(e) As an outside boat, if you claim to have broken an overlap, the onus of proof is on you, that you did so prior to reaching the two lengths circle.

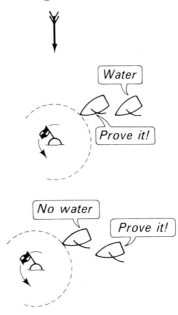

(c) Don't forget that the onus of proof, if there is a collision, falls on the boat which first calls ' water' or 'no water'.

(f) You can only establish an overlap between a yacht and a continuing obstruction such as a shore if at the time there is room to pass between them safely.

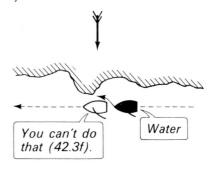

(d)

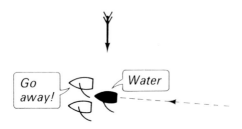

(e) You may only pass between if, when the overlap is established, you can get through safely.

42.4 At a starting mark surrounded by navigable water

When approaching the line to start, a leeward yacht does not have to give a windward yacht room to pass between her and the mark.

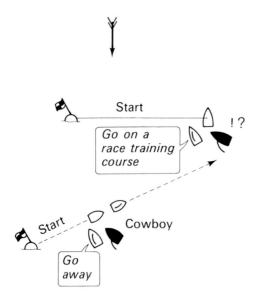

(a) Before the starting signal, *Black* is not entitled to room at the mark.

After the starting signal the leeward yacht shall not deprive the windward yacht of room by sailing above a proper course for the first mark or above a close hauled course, or above the compass course for the first mark (if given).

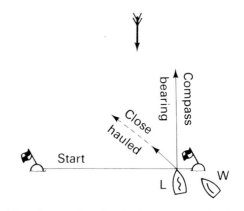

(b) After the starting signal, *L* must not sail above close hauled or the compass bearing for the first mark to keep *W* out. As long as *L* fulfils this and there is still no room, *W* cannot call for water.

RULE 43: CLOSE HAULED, HAILING FOR ROOM TO TACK AT OBSTRUCTIONS

43.1. Hailing

When two yachts are sailing close hauled on the same tack and the yacht clear ahead and/or to leeward has to tack to clear an obstruction, but cannot do so without hitting the windward yacht, she shall hail the other yacht for room to tack, but shall not hail and tack simultaneously.

43.2. Responding

The hailed yacht, at the earliest possible moment after the hail, shall *either:*

(a) Tack–in which case the hailing yacht shall begin to tack either:

- before the hailed yacht has completed her tack;
- if she cannot tack without hitting the hailed yacht, immediately she is able to do so.

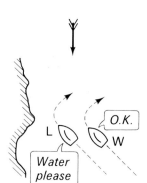

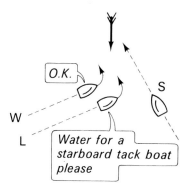

(a) L must commence her tack before W completes hers, or as soon as she can without hitting W.

(c) Should L choose to bear way, she must give W water around the stern of S.

or:

(b) Reply, 'You tack'—when in her opinion she can keep clear without tacking, or after postponing her tack. In this case:

- the hailing yacht shall immediately tack;
- the hailed yacht shall keep clear;
- the onus of satisfying the race committee that she kept clear shall lie on the hailed yacht which replied 'You tack'.

43.3. Limitation on rights to room when the obstruction is a mark

When the hailed yacht can fetch an obstruction which is also a mark, the hailing yacht shall not be entitled to room to tack and clear the obstruction and the hailed yacht shall tell her so. If the hailing yacht calls again, she shall be given room to tack and then must retire or act in accordance with the Sailing Instructions.

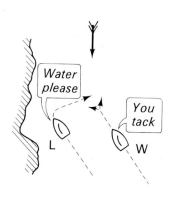

(b) W must now keep clear of L. This is another occasion when starboard gives way to port.

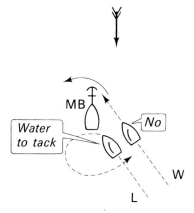

(a) L is not entitled to water unless she calls twice, then she must retire or accept a penalty. L should foresee this situation developing, slow down and tack or gybe. (MB = Mark boat.)

If, having refused the hailing yacht room, the hailed yacht fails to lay the mark, she too will have to retire or act in accordance with the sailing instructions.

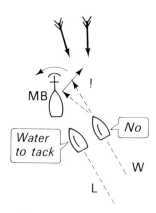

(b) *W* having refused *L* room to tack, subsequently fails to make the mark, due to a backing windshift She must now retire or accept a penalty.

RULE 44: RETURNING TO START

44.1.

After the starting signal is made, a premature starter returning to start, or a yacht working into position from the course side of the line, shall keep clear of yachts which are starting or have started correctly.

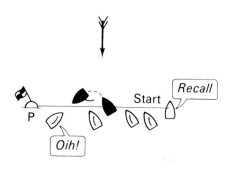

(a) *Black*, a premature starter, now returning to start, must keep clear of the port tack boat (*P*). This is another occasion when starboard gives way to port.

Thereafter she shall be accorded the rights under the rules of *Part IV*, of a yacht which is starting correctly; but when she thereby requires right of way over another yacht which is starting correctly, she shall allow that yacht ample room and opportunity to keep clear.

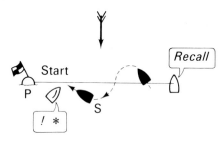

(b) Once *Black* regains her rights, she must allow *P* room and opportunity to keep clear. (Also Rule 35 b i.) Yet again starboard gives way to port.

44.2.

A yacht starting prematurely shall be given the rights of *Part IV* until it is obvious that she is returning to start correctly.

RULE 45: RE-ROUNDING AFTER TOUCHING A MARK

Whilst re-rounding, having touched a mark, you must keep clear of boats rounding correctly, until you are on a proper course for the next mark. Likewise a yacht continuing the course having touched a mark shall be given the rights under *Part IV* until it is obvious she is returning to re-round the mark.

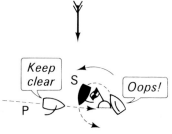

Black, having hit the mark and having to re-round it, must keep clear. Here again, starboard gives way to port.

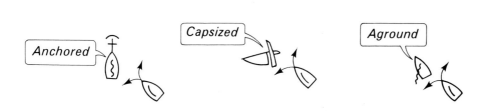

You will not be penalised for touching either a yacht you are assisting which might be in distress, or for touching a yacht which runs aground or capsizes immediately ahead of you. In the above examples, the yachts are racing.

RULE 46: ANCHORED, AGROUND OR CAPSIZED

Under way, you must keep clear of a yacht either anchored, aground or capsized. Of two anchored yachts, the one which anchors last or which is dragging anchor must keep clear of the other.

You must indicate to another yacht your predicament if she is going to foul you—a hail will do. You will not be penalised for fouling a yacht which you are trying to assist, or one which capsizes or runs aground immediately ahead of you.

Finally the Appendices of the Racing Rules contain valuable information, and a good working knowledge of these is also worth acquiring. These Appendices cover the following topics:

1. Amateur Status.
2. Pumping, Rocking and Ouching.
3. Alternative Penalties.
4. Team Racing Rules.
5. Olympic Scoring System.
6. Protest Procedures.
7. Protest Form.
8. Terms of Reference of an International Jury.
9. Conditions for Decisions of an International Jury or Protest Committee.
10. Weighing of Wet Clothing.
11. Authority and Responsibility of Race Committee and Jury for Rule Enforcement.
12. Organisation of Principal Events.

PART 2
RYA Race Training Organisation

10
Structure of the RYA

A young sailor who starts sailing and racing within a Club should ideally come under the guidance of the Club's Race Trainer and should then follow a logical progression of coaching through a racing career. Unfortunately we see far too many youngsters going through an illogical process. They are either directed by parents into the wrong class for their weight or they start off by sailing a dinghy which they are incapable of handling in the medium to strong wind range. Modern dinghies place specific demands on height and body-weight if they are to be successfully raced at National level and above. The pages which follow will point the way for those who want to 'have a go'

Fig. 57 *(see page 124)*, shows the classes of boat which form a logical progression through a racing career.

In these designated classes, physical characteristics, strength and body-weight dictate how long young sailors should spend in any one class.

CATAMARANS

For those who want to move into catamarans there are really only four classes suitable for young sailors. These are as follows:

The Unicorn is the singlehander.

The Dart makes an exciting first boat and has good class structure.

The Shearwater is the longest established, therefore second-hand boats are cheap.

The Tornado is the ultimate racing catamaran and is the Olympic boat.

The age of entry into catamarans for a young sailor is around fifteen years. As a guide, if a crew is heavy enough to sail a 420, then he or she is ready to start in catamarans.

RYA Race Training Structure

Once embarked on a structured racing career, it is important to adopt a training programme under the direction of a Club Race Trainer and then progress along lines suggested by Fig. 58 *(see page 125)*.

There are four main levels of trainer, as follows:

- Club Race Trainers
- Regional Race Training Co-ordinators (RRTC)
- Area Racing Coaches
- National Racing Coach

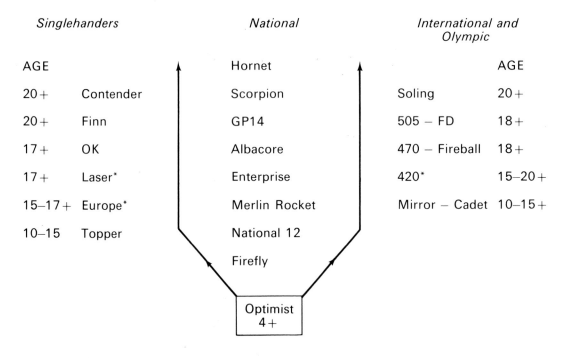

Singlehanders		National	International and Olympic	
AGE		Hornet		AGE
20+	Contender	Scorpion	Soling	20+
20+	Finn	GP14	505 – FD	18+
17+	OK	Albacore	470 – Fireball	18+
17+	Laser*	Enterprise	420*	15–20+
15–17+	Europe*	Merlin Rocket	Mirror – Cadet	10–15+
10–15	Topper	National 12		
		Firefly		
		Optimist 4+		

Note: * used for National and World Youth Championships

Fig. 57.
Dinghy classes and classification.

CLUB RACE TRAINERS

Club Race Trainers, appointed by the Club Training Committee, are responsible for race training for both youths and adults.

Once appointed, a Club Race Trainer will need to organise Introductory and Intermediate race training courses, and must set up the training programme within his or her local environment. The following examples of course programmes use *The RYA National Race Training Scheme* publication *G21/82* as a guideline:

• a five day course, Monday-Friday (good for youth training courses during school holidays);

• two long weekends, Friday evening— Sunday evening;

• two weeks—evenings only;

• weekend sessions—three/four per annum.

The equipment required by a Club Race Trainer is as follows:

1. training area afloat;
2. coaching boat;
3. six portable racing marks (minimum);
4. rescue boat/s;
5. visual starting signals;
6. whistle;
7. changing rooms;
8. lecture room;
9. overhead projector;
10. slide projector;
11. screen;
12. chalkboard.

When organising a race training programme, the Club Race Trainer can call upon the assistance of the Regional Race Training Co-ordinator for outside help in the coaching field and also for any youth race training badges, required to give to young sailors on completion of the course.

The aim of the Club Race Trainer is to raise the standards of racing within the Club. This is achieved by improving the following:

- boat-handling ability
- boat tuning
- starting ability
- tactics
- protest procedures
- racing rules

The training aspects above should be combined with a thorough discussion at the end of each session afloat.

The Club Race Trainer can determine the number of lectures to be prepared for a race training course either by using the RYA publication *G21/82* or by obtaining the services of an Area Racing Coach through the Regional Race Training Co-ordinator.

Fig. 58.
RYA Race Training Structure.

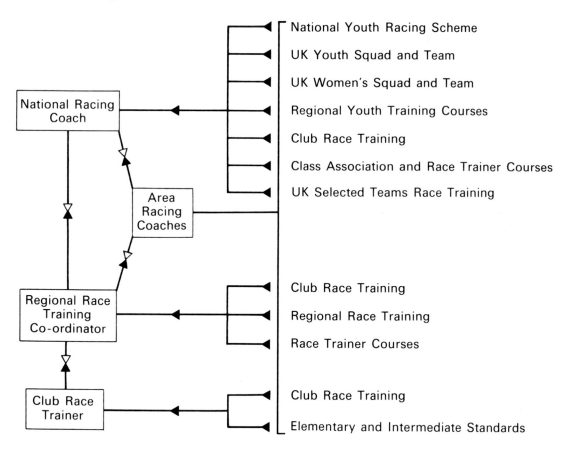

National Youth Racing Scheme

UK Youth Squad and Team

UK Women's Squad and Team

Regional Youth Training Courses

Club Race Training

Class Association and Race Trainer Courses

UK Selected Teams Race Training

National Racing Coach

Area Racing Coaches

Club Race Training

Regional Race Training

Race Trainer Courses

Regional Race Training Co-ordinator

Club Race Training

Elementary and Intermediate Standards

Club Race Trainer

Any general advice or assistance required can be obtained from the Regional Race Training Co-ordinators, or the RYA National Racing Coach.

REGIONAL RACE TRAINING CO-ORDINATORS (RRTC)

The RRTCs are key people in the race training structure who, through the RYA Regional Committee, advise clubs and organisations within their region.

They are responsible to the RYA National Racing Coach for the following:

1. Organising and advising clubs about a race training programme for either youths or adults.
2. Arranging regional youth race training courses.
3. Organising race trainer courses.
4. Arranging for Area Racing Coaches to assist Clubs with race training courses.

AREA RACING COACHES

Area Racing Coaches are selected from well-known, expert sailors and manufacturers who are prepared to put their expertise back into the sport at organised race training sessions. These people are prepared to work at Club, Regional and National levels of race training.

A list of Area Racing Coaches is kept by each RRTC and also by the RYA National Racing Coach.

NATIONAL RACING COACH

There is only one RYA National Racing Coach who is responsible to the RYA Racing Manager for the following:

- National Youth Racing Scheme
- UK Youth Squad and Team
- UK Women's Squad and Team
- Regional Youth Training Courses
- Club Race Training
- Class Association and Race Trainer Courses
- UK Selected Teams Race Training

The National Racing Coach, given plenty of notice, will assist on any race training programme.

The National Youth Racing Scheme

A RRTC and a Club Race Trainer must be fully conversant with the scheme and the basic structure required to organise a race training programme whether it be for youths or adults.

AIMS OF THE SCHEME

1. To raise the standards of racing within the UK at present and in the future.
2. To provide the facilities for the younger generation to improve their personal performance.
3. To seek out and develop individual talent nationally and encourage competition nationally and internationally.
4. To provide a national structure of youth development for both clubs and class associations.
5. To provide a sound base from which youngsters will enjoy sailing a racing dinghy.

11
Race Training Courses

Youth Racing Scheme Organisation

There are three main levels of race training courses in the UK. These are as follows:

CLUB LEVEL

Race training must start at Club level, as already mentioned, under the guidance of the Club Training Committee and the Club Race Trainer. Young sailors showing potential at Club level should be recommended to the RRTC for a regional course.

REGIONAL LEVEL

Courses are organised at Regional level by the RRTC at Intermediate and Advanced levels of race training. Sailors within the region may attend those courses recommended by their Club Race Trainers and Club Training Committee. Those who show potential on these courses will be recommended to the National Racing Coach for a National Youth Racing Course or National Squad training.

NATIONAL LEVEL

Courses will be organised, under the supervision of the National Racing Coach, at National level in England, Scotland, Wales and Northern Ireland. The National Racing Coach will be assisted by RRTCs. Young sailors wishing to attend these courses must be recommended by their RRTC. Those showing potential will be supported for the National and World Youth Championships and will be recommended to go on to Olympic level, if that is what they wish to do.

Race Training Course Standards

The idea of the race training courses is to give a guide to parents, teachers and race trainers as to the ability of a young sailor. This grading system ensures that the trainees do not attend an unsuitable course.

YOUTH RACING SCHEME BADGES

On the successful completion of a course, badges are issued to young sailors depending on the standard they have achieved. The following list gives the progressive order of badges and their colour codes:

Red   — Introductory Youth Race Training Course

White   — Intermediate Youth Race
               Training Course
Blue   — Advanced Youth Race
               Training Course
Silver   — RYA National Youth
               Squad
Gold   — RYA UK Youth Squad
Yellow   — Club Race Trainer's
               badge

1. *Red badge*

Sailors wishing to attend this course, must have attained a standard of proficiency equivalent to the RYA Elementary Dayboat Certificate. This is the only time that the Youth Racing Scheme is related to the National Dayboat Proficiency Scheme (RYA Publication G4). The Red badge serves as a guide to the introductory level of racing, covering the basics of the sport.

2. *White badge*

Sailors attending this course must have either attended the Red badge course or been racing for at least two full seasons.

3. *Blue badge*

Before attending an advanced training course, a sailor must have either attended the Red and White badge courses or have been racing for at least three full seasons. They must also be recommended by their Club Race Trainer and/or RRTC.

4. *Silver badge*

The Silver is awarded to a sailor who attends the RYA National Youth Squad winter training programme, and must also be recommended by their RRTC.

5. *Gold badge*

The Gold is awarded to a sailor who

qualifies for the RYA UK Youth Squad through each of the four National Championships (England, Scotland, Wales and Northern Ireland) and who goes forward to the UK Youth Trials for selection for the World Youth Championship.

6. *Yellow badge*

A Yellow badge is awarded to RYA Race Trainers who attend an RYA Race Trainers Course. On qualifying for the badge they are able to work at Club level. They work under the guidance of the Club Training Committee. Candidates must be experienced racing sailors who know their subject well enough to talk about it and who can pass their knowledge on to others. It is not necessary to be an Olympic Gold Medallist, World, or National Champion to be a good Club Race Trainer.

There are no examinations on the badge courses. The badges are awarded on progressive merit, and faults are corrected during the course either afloat or in the frequent debriefing sessions. These courses are aimed at improving individual performance.

In order to receive the Red, White and Blue badge, and also the Yellow badge, the trainee must attend a race training course in each case. The Silver and Gold badge however, are awarded as the result of selection for the RYA National Youth Squad and, in the case of the Gold badge, selection for the RYA UK Youth Squad.

RACE TRAINING RECORD CARD

This is issued to RYA Junior Members to record their badge scheme progress and their membership of the National Youth Squad or the National Youth Team (Fig. 59).

ROYAL YACHTING ASSOCIATION | NATIONAL YOUTH RACING SCHEME

NAME ....

ADDRESS ....

....

1ST CHANGE OF ADDRESS ....

....

2ND CHANGE ....

....

RECORD CARD

This is to certify that the holder has attained the following Grades:-

RED BADGE
INTRODUCTION TO RACING

Club...

AFFIX
RED BADGE
SEAL AND
OVERSIGN

WHITE BADGE
INTERMEDIATE RACING

Club...

AFFIX
WHITE BADGE
SEAL AND
OVERSIGN

BLUE BADGE
ADVANCED RACING

Club...

AFFIX
BLUE BADGE
SEAL AND
OVERSIGN

IMPORTANT NOTE

THE RYA NATIONAL YOUTH RACING SCHEME IS OPEN TO THOSE WHO ARE FULLY PAID UP JUNIOR MEMBERS OF THE ROYAL YACHTING ASSOCIATION.

YOU WILL BE ASKED TO PRODUCE YOUR CURRENT JUNIOR MEMBERSHIP CARD WHENEVER YOU ENROL FOR A COURSE OR WHEN A BADGE IS AWARDED.

☐ NATIONAL YOUTH SQUAD
☐ NATIONAL YOUTH TEAM

RYA
STAMP

Royal Yachting Association, Victoria Way, Woking

Fig. 59.
RYA National Youth Racing Scheme Record Card.

COURSE REPORTS

On completion of a race training course at Club level, the Club Race Trainer must write a short report about the course including the names of young sailors showing potential. A copy of this (together with recommendations for Regional race training courses), is sent to the RRTC and the Club Training Committee.

Courses at Regional level work in a similar way. The RRTC in charge sends a report to the Chairman of the Regional Training Committee for information and also to the National Racing Coach with the names of those recommended for a National race training course.

The National Racing Coach assists and guides top crews as required, and the records of their progress are kept in a National Register at the RYA office.

RYA Junior Membership

Sailors attending RYA race training courses at Club level must be RYA Junior Members. Those who are not, will be asked to join before they are issued with course material. Those eligible for RYA Junior Membership are young sailors up to and including twenty-one years of age. The cost of the annual subscription is £2.50. (This figure is relevant to 1982 and would be approximately one-third of the cost of the adult subscription.) RYA Junior Members are also entitled to a number of benefits. These are as follows:

- RYA and National Youth race training courses
- Race Training Record Card and Badges
- Access to the RYA for advice and assistance
- RYA Insurance Scheme
- Free allocation of RYA publications
- Access to RYA insignia and goods
- Access to RYA Youth Racing T-Shirts
- Access to RYA Youth Discount Scheme

RYA Youth Discount Scheme

This scheme is available only through the RYA National Racing Coach from the RYA office. It is supported by manufacturers of hulls, spars, sails, fittings, compasses and clothing. The scheme is designed to assist the top young sailors progressing through the Youth Racing Scheme by providing the best available equipment as cheaply as possible.

RYA Toppers

The RYA at present administers thirty-six Toppers which are based around England to be used for youth race training purposes only. There are six trailer-loads which are available for use at Club level, should Trainers wish to use them for training young sailors who do not have their own boats. Club Race Trainers should contact the RRTC with a view to booking and hiring the Toppers. The cost of hire is kept to a minimum weekly fee. The RYA office have details of current costs.

12
Course Preparation and Techniques of Instruction

Course Preparation

The Club Race Trainier must prepare a training programme prior to the course. Preparation is two-thirds of the battle and forms the basis of a smoothly run course. When planning a race training course the following must be considered:

1. *Venue*
This must be chosen bearing the following in mind:

(a) Shore side facilities:
- lecture room;
- changing facilities;
- ramp or area for launching and recovering boats.

(b) Facilities afloat:
The training area should be free of strong tides and away from busy traffic routes. This will make it easier for the Club Race Trainer to control the group and safer for the sailors themselves.

2. *Advertising*
An important part of a training programme is to advertise the course. In the case of a course arranged for a Club and its members, this can be done by newsletter and a notice on the Club notice-board. If the Club Race Trainer wishes to extend the course and invite neighbouring club members to attend, the advertising must be extended considerably, and even more so at Regional and National level.

Communication in sailing is a major problem, people do not read notices unless they are pointed out to them. The advertising must be done thoroughly and organised well before the planned date of the course—four or five weeks beforehand is too late!

3. *Boats and pupils*
On a five day race training course the ideal situation is as follows:

(a) Boats:
- one class of boat (class association training)
- two, three or four classes of boats with even numbers (for pair, match and team racing exercises).

(b) Pupils:
Here the Club Race Trainer must work

within his or her own parameters, but as an example, one Trainer can cater for thirty pupils over a five day period. The more Trainers working together, the more candidates can be accepted for the course.

4. *Lectures*

G21/82 RYA publication can be used purely as a guide to prepare lectures for the course. Lectures on Boat Tuning, Racing Rules and Tactics are all part of the course and it is important to plan the depth of treatment each of these and any other topics carefully so that they are suited to the particular course and are gauged at the right level. Careful planning is essential, whether the lectures are to be given by the Club Race Trainer or by an outside speaker imported for the occasion.

5. *Safety afloat*

Safety afloat is always of paramount importance but particularly when it involves young sailors.

Essential points to consider are:

(a) Clothing:
Pupils must be wearing the correct clothing for the conditions prevailing on the day. On warm days, it is essential that sailing clothing can be opened at the neck and/or down the front of the garment, to allow the heat to evaporate from the body so as to prevent over-heating which can be just as dangerous as over-cooling.

On cold days and when water temperatures sink below 40°F—nine months of the year in the UK—a wet suit is essential. It also helps to wear Thermal wear under a wet suit to afford some form of ventilation, and it is important to wear windproof clothing over the wet suit. A woolly hat or head gear of some sort, worn during the colder months from November to May, helps to retain 40–50% of the body heat which would otherwise be lost.

(b) Rescue Boats:
When deciding on the number of rescue craft, the weather conditions on the day as well as the number of boats on the water should be taken into consideration. Always plan for the worst possible situation and ensure that the group is adequately covered.

6. *Portable racing marks*

At least six portable racing marks will be required during a training programme. These are relatively easy to make up and should be made so that they are easy to transport, both afloat and ashore.

7. *Protest procedures*

During a race training course the subject of Protests and that of the Racing Rules must be covered. It goes without saying that the Club Race Trainer must be familiar with both of these in order to teach them correctly.

During the latter part of the course, it is good practice to select an 'incident' and elect a 'protest committee' from within the course. The Club Race Trainer can monitor the protest to see that it is run smoothly and that the correct decision is arrived at.

8. *Physical fitness training*

This is covered practically on the Advanced race training course each morning before breakfast. The object of this session is to give the pupils a practical pattern of training which they should be encouraged to do every day for at least three months prior to a major event, not three days or even worse, three hours before a race—it is too little and too late then! The Trainer must be prepared to participate in these sessions, or if unable to do so, should import the expertise.

It cannot be stressed enough that careful pre-course preparation is essential to the success of the coures.

Techniques of Instruction

Those who would like to take on the task of being a Club Race Trainer but feel they have little or no experience of lecturing should consider attending a course in techniques of instruction as the best way to start on the right path.

Some people have a natural ability to stand in front of a group and impart information without any obvious difficulty. However, anyone not endowed with this ability can quickly learn the basic skills required to give a satisfactory and workmanlike lecture.

The following points provide basic guidelines for those wishing to embark on or improve their lecture techniques:

1. *Preparation*
There is no substitute for careful planning. The subject to be covered should be carefully considered and, the depth to which it is to be covered, the time allowed and the method of presentation, should be looked at as a whole, prior to the lecture.

2. *Knowledge of the subject*
It is foolish to embark upon a lecture if you are not fully conversant with the subject. It is important to know the subject matter in detail, which gives you the confidence to stand up in front of a group and not only deliver the subject matter effectively but answer any questions that might arise from the talk.

3. *Structure of the lecture*
The lecture itself has three basic components:

(a) Introduction:
   This explains the relevance and importance of the subject matter to the course as a whole.
(b) The Topic:
   This is the main part of the lecture, where the essential facts are explained. It is important to aim the subject matter at the right level, not to lose sight of that level and to present the material in a logical sequence so that all the relevant details are covered within the allocated time.
(c) Conclusion:
   This is a summary of the lecture which should help to highlight and drive home the salient points.

4. *Question and answer techniques*
It is important, particularly when dealing with an audience of young sailors, to make them feel involved, and having gained their interest and attention, to keep it. An effective way of achieving this is through 'questions and answers'. Whether questions are put to the audience during the lecture, or dealt with at the end of the time allocated to the topic, will depend on the individual, the time and length of the lecture, the depth of the subject matter and the ability of the students. However this technique is used, it is an excellent way to involve an audience and to 're-cap' on the information given.

Aim the question at the group, let them all ponder on the answer and only ask an individual when everyone has had time to formulate an answer.

5. *Visual Aids*

Each lecturer develops a technique and method of presentation. Whatever style is used, visual aids can be most helpful in getting the subject matter over to the students. These aids can be an overhead projector, slides, video, polaroid camera, tape recorder, films, models, magnetic board, chalkboard, printed material, notes or diagrams. The lecturer should consider the best form of visual aid suitable for the particular lecture. Its use should be clearly relevant and it should be presented at the right time.

The following are examples of the proper use of visual aids:

(a) Films:
   The lecturer should see the film first before showing it to students. The content of the film should be outlined without ruining the viewing, and the lecturer should suggest to the audience the points they should be looking for and the areas to be discussed later. After viewing the film, it should be discussed using the 'question and answer' technique and if necessary and if time allows, the film can be shown again so that with the newly acquired knowledge, it may be better understood and remembered.

(b) Chalkboard:
   This is one of the oldest of the visual aids and is still very effective, not being subject to mechanical breakdowns. Simple though it is to use, there are some important points to remember. These are as follows:

   • Do not write on the board, facing away from the students, while talking at the same time.
   • It is better to write on the board first, then turn round and talk about it.
   • It is better still if possible, to prepare the material and write it on the board before the lecture, and then talk about it.
   • The whole chalkboard should be used if necessary.
   • Writing must be neat and legible.
   • Coloured chalks help to make different points stand out, though the use of too many at a time can be confusing.

(c) Tape Recorder:
   This is very useful for making 'notes' afloat, and comments on the performance of boats and crews. Once ashore, the tape can be replayed and the comments discussed with the group or individual.

(d) Video:
   The use of video equipment is good for recording boat handling techniques, tacking, gybing, spinnaker work, mark rounding, starting but will only prove useful if handled by a skilled operator.

(e) Polaroid Camera:
   This is useful for illustrating points on boat tuning, leach shapes, slot shapes, and mast rake etc., after a session afloat.

An important fact to bear in mind is that any aid is only as good as the person using it. The operator must be skilled in the use of whatever equipment he or she is handling.

6. *Room Environment*

The area or room in which the lecture is to be given is often one over which the lecturer has no control but whenever and wherever possible, the room should be set up to the best advantage. The group should be oriented in the room correctly, and the source of light, entry and exit points, plug sockets, blackout facilities, ventilation etc. all considered. These must be checked beforehand so that the Lecturer is not caught unprepared.

7. *Guide Notes*

Only the very experienced lecturer should give a talk without using notes. Otherwise, lecture notes should always be prepared carefully. It is not a good policy, however, to walk around the room reading the lecture directly from the notes. This does not inspire confidence and instead suggests an insufficient knowledge of the subject. The notes should be written prior to the lecture with the main headings underlined, and should be referred to by the lecturer from time to time.

8. *Voice and Mannerisms*

A vital point when giving a lecture is that the lecturer's voice must be heard by the students sitting furthest away. It is important to learn to project the voice to every corner, because if it cannot be heard distinctly, the audience will soon lose interest. Personal mannerisms are part of everyone's make-up. Often they add character and individuality to the style of a lecturer but if they are bad one, (a friend or enemy will give advice on this!) they can be very distracting and it is better to try to eliminate them.

The points outlined above are by no means revolutionary, but they may not be immediately obvious to those giving lectures for the first time.

13
RYA Race Training Exercises

The twenty courses shown and explained below are used by the RYA to highlight particular aspects of racing which need constant practising.

1. Olympic Course

Used for the first practical session afloat to ascertain the general standard of the group, and to lay the foundations from which to start coaching having noted the good and bad points. This exercise is also used for subsequent individual races during the training sessions.

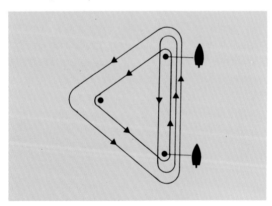

2. 'E' Type Exercise

Good exercise for improving the gybing technique. The three gybe marks are laid so as to allow the crews sufficient time to gybe, settle down and have to consider gybing again. The distance between marks varies with the wind strength and the type of boat on the course. This course can be used to run a race, or for a follow–the–leader exercise. If it is used for racing, start at the leeward mark and finish at the windward mark as in exercise 1.

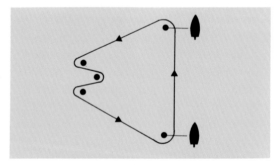

3. Sausage Course

Used specifically for match racing—1 versus 1—and team racing 2 v. 2 or 3 v. 3. This is introduced later in the course, on day three or four, to improve boat handling skills, develop tactics and increase knowledge of the racing rules. Three rounds are normally sailed, having to pass through the start/finish line on the windward leg but allowed to go anywhere on the downwind leg. The distance between marks, as in all training exercises, is relatively short so as to sharpen the crews' wits and keep them alert with a lot of action in a short space of time.

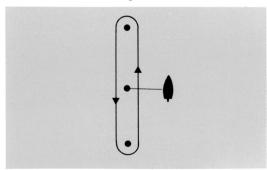

4. Box Course

Purely a boat-handling exercise used in a follow–the–leader situation with the trainer positioned in the middle of the course. The trainer should be looking at the crews' ability to tack well, stipulating 'X' number of tacks up the short windward leg and similarly, gybes on the downwind leg, and he should also be looking at boat balance and trim, sail trim and mark rounding ability. If the crew of any boat has difficulty executing any of these skills, the trainer should call the boat alongside after it has rounded the bottom left hand mark, discuss the problem and feed the boat back around the bottom right hand mark for further practise.

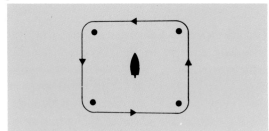

5. Circular Course

Also a boat handling–exercise with particular attention to roll tacking and gybing practised around the trainer so that he can look into the boat and see exactly where the problem might lie. This exercise is most effective with a small group of boats—six or less.

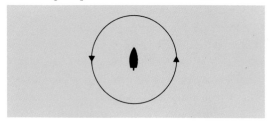

6. Reaching Exercise

In this exercise, the boats gybe round one end and tack round the other. The trainer should be watching for good boat handling, balance and trim, sail trim, tacking and gybing, and mark rounding. Distance between marks should be as is necessary for the number and size of boats and the strength of the wind.

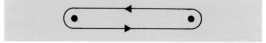

7. Triangle Course

Tactics, boat speed, racing rules and boat handling are all closely looked at in this exercise. The trainer positions himself/ herself to windward and gives the group a starting procedure. When they start, the trainer moves slowly ahead allowing the group to catch up. The group must stay within two imaginary lines between the trainer and the two outer distance marks. As a boat touches this line a whistle is blown and they must tack to stay inside the triangle. If they sail outside the triangle they are disqualified. If there is a boat on their weather quarter they must gybe and pass astern, they cannot call for water on the imaginary line under Rule 43.

As the boats close on the training boat and

the apex of the triangle, tacking becomes more frequent and close-quarter tactical situations develop. When the boats arrive at the training boat, they must treat this as a windward mark and leave it to port.

This exercise brings out deficiencies in skills and tactics and affords plenty of practice to perfect them. The maximum number of boats taking part in this exercise at any one time is about six or seven boats.

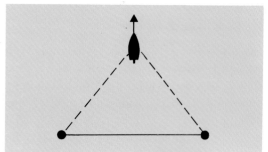

8. Leeward Mark Rounding Practice

This is a running start set with the bias for the outer distance mark. Crews must choose to go for the favoured end or for the inside berth overlap. The trainer should look to see how the group tackles the problem of leeward mark rounding in a large group of boats and how they apply Rule 42!

This is a useful training exercise when combining the same line to finish after rounding the leeward mark.

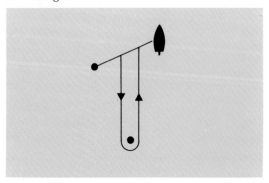

9. Slalom Exercise

A boat-handling exercise to develop roll tacking and gybing techniques. This exercise may be practised either in a single line or in two lanes of buoys lying parallel to each other with a short reach across the top and bottom. With the trainer positioned in the middle and using the follow–the–leader pattern, it is possible to put more boats on to the course and it makes it easier to take out, advise, and return to the exercise, members of the group who need extra advice (as in exercise 4).

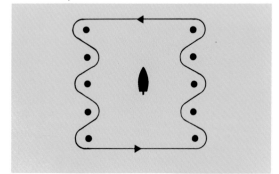

10. Follow–the–Leader Exercise

This exercise aims to improve boat-handling ability and also to make crews aware of how to accelerate and stop the boat in varying wind strengths. It allows crews to learn more about the characteristics of their own boats.

With the training boat as the leader, the group should sail behind it in a straight line, keeping roughly a boat length apart in light to medium wind strength. If an individual boat is unable to maintain its position it must pass the boat in front on either side and tack or gybe and join the end of the line. Young sailors in particular do not like to fall out of line and allow either their fellow sailors to overtake them or let the trainer see that they are not handling their boats properly. This makes them work very hard to very good advantage!

This exercise is very good for improving boat-handling as the group follow the coaching boat tacking and gybing, as if on a slalom course. The trainer can hand the lead over to one of the trainees so that he can observe the exercise from either side.

11. Tacking Exercise

This exercise is most effective with a small group of boats. The boats should start in line abreast, not too close together. They should sail to windward, tacking on the whistle. Those tacking their boats correctly will soon start to move out in front, and when this happens they should be stopped, re-grouped and started again. The boats must aim to keep to their line–a–breast formation during the exercise. The trainer should follow behind the line of boats, looking at each one in turn and sorting out their individual problems.

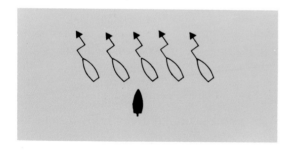

12. Gybing Exercise

As for 11, but downwind this time so that the group may practise and improve their gybing skills in the same manner with or without spinnakers.

13. Starting Exercise

The windward mark should be placed approximately 100 yards from the starting position. If only one group is being trained, they should round the windward mark and sail straight back through the start/finishing line. If there is more than one group, each group should sail a semi-circle back to leeward, keeping clear of the next group making their way up to the windward mark. Whilst the group makes its way to windward the bias of the line should be altered so that each start is different, and the length can also be altered.

The pre-start area can be limited by setting two marks to leeward of the line, one to leeward of the outer distance mark and the other to leeward of the training boat, to form a box. On the warning signal the group must get inside the box and stay there until the start. This makes the sailors think and observe the racing rules, because it duplicates the situation found in a much larger fleet.

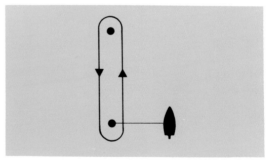

14. Reaching Exercise

A boat handling exercise aimed at improving boat balance, trim, sail trim and gybing ability around two wing marks. The distance between marks depends on the size of boat and prevailing wind speed.

15. Boat Handling Exercise

Used for both single and doublehanders to sharpen up boat-handling and mark rounding ability. Spinnakers should be used during offwind legs.

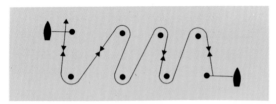

16. Speed Training Exercise

Used for speed runs, timing from line-mark-line. Also numerous courses can be formed for boat handling, mark rounding and tactical exercises, as well as Olympic courses.

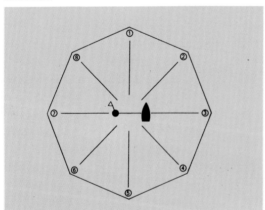

17. Extension of the Olympic Course

As an alternative to the standard Olympic course, this course is used to involve and examine all eleven aspects of the sport, particularly mark rounding practice. Thorough debriefing is necessary.

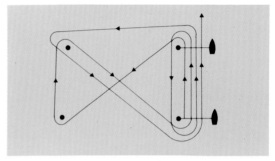

18. Alternative Slalom Course

An extension of exercise No. 9, this exercise is again aimed at advanced boat-handling skill and mark rounding. It can be used either as a follow–the–leader exercise (small group—up to twelve), or as a race.

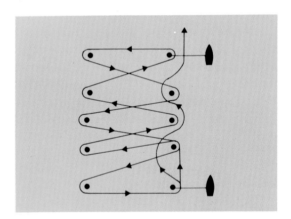

19. Le Mans Race Start

With sails down and boats lined up on the shore alongside each other, this is an individual speed race. Seamanship exercises can also be fed in on each leg of the course, and/or rudderless racing—depending on the number of boats taking part in the exercise and the size of the sailing area! The finish is as for the start.

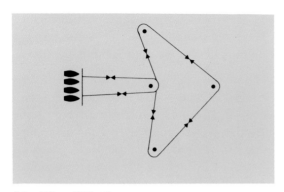

20. The 'X' Course

The 'X' course is used for either individual, match or team racing, covering all aspects of the sport, especially tactics, rules, mark rounding and boat handling.

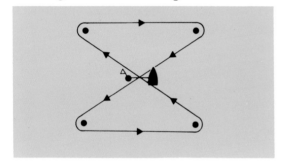

BOAT TUNING RUNS

For crews to gain anything from boat tuning exercises they must:

- work closely with another boat or small group of boats;
- communicate with each other to exchange ideas and thoughts;
- sail other boats so as to be able to look at their own rig from the outside, and get the feel of another boat in comparison to their own.

To achieve this the trainer should seed crews as being compatible to each other in terms of speed through the water, and organise the group in the following manner:

1. Put the crews in pairs as for match racing. Each pair then sails to windward on port or starboard tack, one boat in the safe leeward position slightly ahead, approximately three boat lengths away. One crew then set up their boat as they think fit for the conditions prevailing and sail that boat as fast as possible without any alterations to any of the controls. The second crew are allowed to alter and adjust controls as they wish to see if they can improve their speed and pointing ability.

   If they wish to stop and make alterations, they may do so, they then regroup and go off again. If the two boats sail too far from each other they must stop the exercise, re-group and start again. The object is to move forward in short bursts of approximately 4-500 yards.

   Once in the windward area the two boats run back down to leeward alongside each other, on opposite tacks, discussing what they have achieved and comparing notes on adjustments made.

2. When they arrive back in the leeward area, they start the exercise again. This time the boat which was free to alter its controls becomes the 'static' boat, giving the other boat the opportunity to experiment.

   Again on completion of the first leg, the boats run down to leeward as before and exchange thoughts and ideas as to how to improve on their speed, etc.

3. Crews change over into the other boats for the third run up and repeat the exercise. This is the best and quickest way to improve on boat speed and pointing ability.

Having practised boat tuning in pairs, the trainer can put three pairs together with a 'wing' boat who will call out instructions as to when to stop, re-group and when to make any alterations. Much progress can be made working together in this way, each boat gaining from the experience and expertise of the others.

STARTING PROCEDURES FOR RACE TRAINING
EXERCISES

1. *Sound signals*

A whistle is used for race training as follows:

- 1 short blast—turn 90° to Starboard from present course.
- 2 short blasts—turn 90° to Port from present course.
- 1 long blast—hoist or lower spinnaker.
- Series of short blasts—stop what you are doing and observe approaching hazard.

These sound signals are very useful for exercise 10, the follow-the-leader exercise when, on a beam reach, the trainer wants to turn the crews on to a run for spinnaker work. It is also very useful for tacking practice as in exercise 11, and for gybing in exercise 12.

2. *Visual signals*

The simplest visual aid for crews is a 'training stick', made by bolting together three battens at their lower edge. Opened out they signal 3-2-1 minutes as required. Flags or three number boards can also be used.

Appendices

Appendix I : Race Training Format

Day	Class Room	Afloat	Class Room	Afloat	Class Room	
1	Introduction Discussion Briefing	Exercise 1 (twice round) Exercise 10	Debrief Discussion Briefing	Boat handling exercises. Exercises 4, 5, 9, 10, 11 and 12	Debrief Discussion	Lecture: How to improve your racing
2	Lecture: Starting techniques and ability	Starting practice 1. Fixed start 2. Gate start Exercise 13 (Fixed)	As above	Spinnaker work Exercise 3, 6, 8, 10 and 12 Boat handling exercise Individual racing Exercise 2	As above	Lecture: Tactics
3	Lecture: Racing Rules	Exercise 3. (match racing: 1 versus 1)	As above	Exercise 3 (team racing: 2 versus 2)	As above	Lecture: Boat tuning
4	Practical demonstration ashore: Boat tuning	Boat tuning in pairs Exercise 13	As above	Boat tuning in groups Exercise 11 and 13	As above	Lecture: Compass work and windshift tracking
5	Lecture: Meteorology	Windshift tracking Individual racing Exercise 1, 2, and 13	As above	Exercise 1. (Race full Olympic course)	As above	Wash-up Departure

Appendix II : Physical Fitness Standards

A performance chart for men and for women, to indicate the level of fitness to be achieved for success in the sport.

Men

1.5 Mile Run

(Optional alternative to 2 mile walk for those aged 45 or over.)

Age		under 30	30 – 34	35-39	40 – 44	45 – 49	50 – 54
Times for	1	12.01 – 14.30	12.31 – 15.00	13.01 – 15.30	13.31 – 16.00	14.01 – 16.30	14.31 – 17.00
Levels	2	11.01 – 12.00	11.31 – 12.30	12.01 – 13.00	12.06 – 13.30	12.46 – 14.00	13.16 – 14.30
(Minutes and	3	10.16 – 11.00	10.38 – 11.30	11.01 – 12.00	11.16 – 12.05	11.31 – 12.45	12.01 – 13.15
Seconds)	4	Under 10.16	Under 10.38	Under 11.01	Under 11.16	Under 11.31	Under 12.01

2 Mile Walk

(Optional alternative to 1.5 mile run for those aged 45 or over)

Age		45 – 49	50 – 54	55 and over
Times for	1	29.31 – 35.07	31.16 – 37.00	33.01 – 38.45
Levels	2	27.31 – 29.30	29.16 – 31.15	31.01 – 33.00
(Minutes and	3	26.16 – 27.30	27.16 – 29.15	29.01 – 31.00
Seconds)	4	Under 26.16	Under 27.16	Under 29.01

Level 1 = Poor

Level 2 = Satisfactory

Level 3 = Good

Level 4 = Very Good

Level 2 is the minimum level to aim for.

750 Yard Swim

Age		under 30	30 – 34	35-39	40 – 44	45 – 49	50 – 54
Times for	1	16.31 – 19.00	17.16 – 19.45	18.01 – 20.30	18.46 – 21.15	19.31 – 22.00	20.16 – 22.45
Levels	2	15.16 – 16.30	16.01 – 17.15	16.46 – 18.00	17.31 – 18.45	18.16 – 19.30	19.01 – 20.15
(Minutes and	3	14.01 – 15.15	14.46 – 16.00	15.31 – 16.45	16.16 – 17.30	17.01 – 18.15	17.46 – 19.00
Seconds)	4	Under 14.01	Under 14.46	Under 15.31	Under 16.16	Under 17.01	Under 17.46

Women

1.5 Mile Run

(Optional alternative to 2 mile walk for those aged 45 or over.)

Age		under 30	30 – 34	35-39	40 – 44	45 – 49	50 – 54
Times for	1	14.31 – 17.30	15.01 – 18.00	15.31 – 18.30	16.01 – 19.00	16.31 – 19.30	17.01 – 20.00
Levels	2	13.31 – 14.30	14.01 – 15.00	14.31 – 15.30	15.01 – 16.00	15.31 – 16.30	16.01 – 17.00
(Minutes and	3	12.31 – 13.30	13.01 – 14.00	13.31 – 14.30	14.01 – 15.00	14.31 – 15.30	15.01 – 16.00
Seconds)	4	Under 12.31	Under 13.01	Under 13.31	Under 14.01	Under 14.31	Under 15.01

2 Mile Walk

(Optional alternative to 1.5 mile run for those aged 45 or over)

Age		45 – 49	50 – 54	55 and over
Times for	1	35.46 – 42.30	37.31 – 44.15	39.16 – 46.00
Levels	2	33.46 – 35.45	35.31 – 37.30	37.16 – 39.15
(Minutes and	3	31.46 – 33.45	33.31 – 35.30	35.16 – 37.15
Seconds)	4	Under 31.46	Under 33.31	Under 35.16

Level 1 = Poor

Level 2 = Satisfactory

Level 3 = Good

Level 4 = Very Good

Level 2 is the minimum level to aim for.

750 Yard Swim

Age		under 30	30 – 34	35-39	40 – 44	45 – 49	50 – 54
Times for	1	20.01 – 23.00	21.31 – 24.30	23.01 – 26.00	24.31 – 27.30	26.01 – 29.00	27.31 – 30.30
Levels	2	18.31 – 20.00	20.01 – 21.30	21.31 – 23.00	23.01 – 24.30	24.31 – 26.00	26.01 – 27.30
(Minutes and	3	17.01 – 18.30	18.31 – 20.00	20.01 – 21.30	21.31 – 23.00	23.01 – 24.30	24.31 – 26.00
Seconds)	4	Under 17.01	Under 18.31	Under 20.01	Under 21.31	Under 23.01	Under 24.31

Appendix III : Boat Tuning Log

This is an important log for evaluating equipment and for boat tuning. It is used to record sheeting positions, rig tension, mast ram, mast rake, kicker tension, board and cunningham hole position etc. for various sea states and wind strengths.

Date of Race. . . . .   *Venue*. . . . .

	Beating			
	Reaching			
	Running			
	Type:			
M A I N S A I L	Cunningham			
	Clew Outhaul			
	Kicker Tension			
	Mast Ram			
	Traveller Position			
	Mainsheet Position			
	Type:			
J I B	Barber Hauler			
	Sheet Lead Block			
	Cunningham			
	Halyard Position			
	Sheet Position			
	Type:			
S P I N N A K E R	Pole Height			
	Halyard Position			
	Sheet Position			
	Luff Curl			
	Leach Twist			
	Foot Shape			
Centreboard Position				
Rudder Blade Position				

Sea State
Wind Strength
Mask Rake
Shroud Tension
Jib Luff Tension
Spreader Length
Spreader Angle
Mast Bend
Mast Heel Position

Remarks:

_____
_____
_____
_____
_____
_____
_____
_____
_____
_____

Appendix IV : Windshift Tracking Chart

This is used prior to the start of a race to establish what the wind is doing and which will be the freeing tack off the starting line. The example below shows an oscillating wind around a mean wind direction.

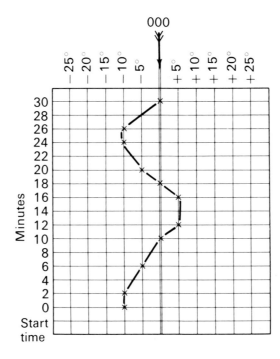

Appendix V : Race Area Information

Data concerning wind and tidal currents across the race area should be gathered together prior to the start of the race, either by a coach or by yourself.

General:

Weather:

Instructions:

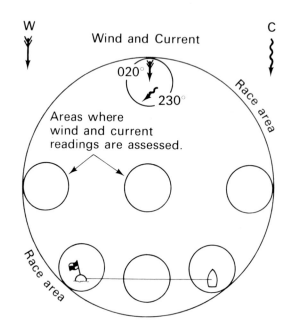

Appendix VI : Starting

A logical approach to making the perfect start.

FIXED LINE START

1. Weather forecast – wind left/right, velocity up/down.
2. Surface current or tide – duration of race.
3. Sea state – duration of race, left and right of course.
4. Sail windward leg – check boat tuning and compass heading.
5. Check line bias during preparatory period, and transits.
6. Select correct end of the line, then decide the following:

    • port/ starboard tack approach
    • pin end/weather side of other sailors (port end)
    • pin end/leeward side of other sailors (starboard end)
    • middle of line on transits.

7. Check speed of approach to line.
8. Check windward and leeward for sail plan coverage.
9. Create space to leeward during final minute.
10. Accelerate with boat on your weather side.
11. Settle down quickly – go for speed and clear air.
12. In shifty conditions, get on to freeing tack quickly.
13. Do not tack in starting area due to confused wind and sea area.
14. Always take the tack which takes you closest to the mark.

GATE START

The same points apply to gate starts as to fixed starts, with a few further considerations. These are as follows:

1. Is the pathfinder faster than you? If so, go late; if slower, go early.
2. Do you want to go left up the beat, if so, go early; if going right up the beat, go later; if going up the middle of the beat, go in the middle.
3. Is the wind shifting left? If so, go early; if it is shifting right, go later.

Appendix VII : Race Analysis

WHY DID I/WE NOT DO WELL?

1. *Technology*
Hull, spars, sails, foils, fittings. Are they good enough?

2. *Boat preparation*
Did anything break – does everything work?

3. *Self preparation*
Are we fit enough physically and mentally? Physical fitness leads to mental fitness which gives confidence.

4. *Geographical, tidal and meteorological preparation*
Did I/we check for any permanent wind bends over the racing area due to surrounding land mass?
Did I/we know the strength and direction of any surface current throughout the race period over the whole course?
Did I/we have the latest weather information and know what the wind was expected to do?

5. *Boat handling ability*
Is our tacking good enough?
Is our gybing good enough (with/without spinnaker)?
Is our spinnaker drill quick enough?
Are we balancing the boat correctly on all points of sailing?
Are we trimming the boat correctly on all points of sailing?
Are we in full control of the boat in all conditions and do we appreciate its handling characteristics?

6. *Was the rig set up correctly for the conditions of the day?*
Was the rig tension correct?
Was the mast rake correct?
Were the spreaders the correct length and angle?
Was the cunningham hole tension correct on all points of sailing?
Was the mast ram set correctly?
Did we have the correct amount of mast bend for the conditions?
Is the mast heel in the correct position?
Is it a tight fit (no twist)?
Was the kicking strap tension correct for all points of sailing?
Was the traveller in the correct position for all points of sailing?
Did I use the main clew outhaul correctly on all points of sailing?
Did we use the barber hauler system correctly?
Was the slot shape correct?

FIXED LINE:
Did I/we select the correct end to start from?
Did I/we check on a transit after preparatory signal?
Was I up near the line at start time going at speed in clear wind?
Was my final approach to the line tactically correct (no-one immediately to leeward of me)?

Was I on the correct tack off the line (shifty conditions)?
Did I infringe any Racing Rules (32; 33; 34; 35; 36; 37; 40; 41; 42.4)?

GATE STARTING:

Did I/we assess speed of the pathfinder?
Did I/we assess wind and tide to go early, middle or late?
(Also check relevant clauses from Fixed Line starting).
Did I concentrate on speed and pointing initially after starting to get away from the opposition?

TACTICS

Did I/we take the tack which took me/us closest to the windward mark?
Did I/we take the tack which took me/us to a nearby shore line (if applicable) first?
Did I stay with the main bunch of the fleet?
Did I use the wind shifts/gusts/bends to advantage?
Was my final approach to windward mark correct?
Did I get to the lay-line too early?
Was I always between the main bunch of the fleet and the next mark?
On the reaching legs, did I get above, on or below the rhumb line for a backing or veering wind or to gain the advantage defending our wind?
On the running leg, did we get left or right of the rhumb line for above reasons?
Did I use my wind indicator to ensure I was on the correct gybe, not sailing by the lee?
Was I on the correct tack during my final approach to leeward mark?
Did we go for the correct end of the finishing line?
Did I use my compass correctly throughout the race?

RACING RULES

Did I use the Rules to my advantage both as my attacking and defending weapon?
Do I know the Rules (in particular 31–46 and 60)?
Am I fully conversant with Protest procedures?

SAILING INSTRUCTIONS

Did I/we read these thoroughly?
Did we take a copy afloat with us?
Did I understand them fully?

Appendix VIII : Protests

Far too many competitors are unsuccessful with their protests because they do not take the trouble to protest properly.

When a protest is not a VALID protest the Protest Committee can do nothing with it. In order to make a protest VALID the following simple requirements have to be satisfied.

1. The appropriate protest flag must have been displayed correctly and kept displayed until finishing. (RULE 68.3 (a) (i)).
   (For singlehanded races–displayed correctly at the incident and on finishing. (RULE 68.3 (a) (ii)).
2. Preferably, the sail number of the boat protested against should be reported to the Race Officer on the finishing vessel. This is often requested but is not usually mandatory. (Sailing Instruction).
3. The protestor must have made an attempt to have informed the protestee that a protest will be lodged. (RULE 68.3 (c)).
4. The protest must be lodged in writing on the form provided (RULE 68.3 (d)) before the end of protest time. (Sailing Instruction).
   When a protest is lodged very close to the end of protest time, it is sometimes a good idea to write the time at which it was lodged on the top of the form. This can be confirmed or corrected by the protest office.
5. The form must be correctly completed. (RULE 68.3 (d)). Provided it includes a "summary of the facts" defects may be remedied later. Without a written "summary of the facts" the protest is useless. (RULE 68.3 (f)).

A protest which satisfies the above requirements will be accepted as a valid protest and heard by the Protest Committee, but having got so far it is also necessary:

1. to make sure of the time and place of the hearing (Notice Board):
2. to attend at the appointed time with your witnesses and wait until you are called. When required by the sailing instructions to make sure that the protestee is aware that a protest has been lodged and will be heard at the time and place appointed.
3. It is always advisable to look at the protest notice board even when you are sure no one will be protesting against you.
4. When either party to the protest fails to attend, the protest will be decided without a full hearing. (RULE 70.3).

INVALID PROTESTS

When a protest is not a valid protest, the Protest Committee cannot take any action on it.

The Protest Committee should post a notice that the protest has not been heard because it was not a valid protest.

Another competitor, who witnessed the infringement, who did not protest because he was satisfied that a protest would be lodged by one of the boats involved, when it is reported that the protest is not a valid protest, may himself lodge a protest against the infringing boat within such time after the report is issued, as the Race Committee considers reasonable. (RULE 68.3 (b)).

It is often asked why the Protest Committee does not take action when it has evidence of alleged infringements from invalid protests. The reason is that the Rules only provide for action to be taken from evidence at the hearing of a VALID protest. (RULE 73.2 (e)).

When there is evidence of any sort that an infringement has resulted in serious damage, action can be taken. (RULE 73.2 (c)).

ALTERNATIVE PENALTIES (Appendix 3)

When one of the alternative penalty systems is being used, the protesting procedure is exactly the same except that:

720° turns (Appendix 3-1)
In addition to displaying the protest flag correctly, the boat infringed against must also "hail" the infringing boat in order to give her the opportunity to exonerate herself by doing her 720° turns. When satisfied that the penalty has been correctly carried out, the protest flag, can be hauled down and no further action is necessary. When the boat infringed against is not satisfied that the infringing boat has carried out the penalty correctly, or when she has suffered serious damage, she will continue to display her protest flag and to lodge a protest.

It is then up to the infringing boat to satisfy the Protest Committee that she did exonerate herself correctly: if not, the protest will proceed in the usual way.

Percentage Penalty (Appendix 3-2)
In this system, also, a protest flag and a "hail" are required to give the infringing boat an opportunity to display an acknowledgment of infringement flag, usually IC flag "I". When IC flag "I" is displayed the protest flag can be hauled down and no further action taken except confirming at the end of protest time that the acknowledgment has been reported. When IC flag "I" is not displayed, or there has been serious damage, the protest procedure will proceed in the usual way.

In some cases the IC flag "I" may be displayed before the protest flag, in which case the boat infringed against need not show a protest flag but must confirm later that the acknowledgment has been reported.

Once IC flag "I" has been displayed it must be displayed until finishing and the acknowledgment of infringement must be reported to the Race Committee, usually to the Protest Office (Appendix 3.2.2.). Special IC flag "I" forms should be provided.

The Race Committee should post details of IC flag "I" acknowledgments on the notice board as soon as possible after the end of protest time, to enable the boats infringed against to confirm that the acknowledgment has been reported.

When it is found that a boat has displayed IC flag "I" and not reported her acknowledgment, this must be reported to the Race Committee and the infringing boat shall then be liable to the maximum percentage penalty without a hearing, except that she may request a hearing on the two points of having displayed IC flag "I" and having reported the acknowledgment.

Appendix IX : Race Trainer Course Programme

DAY 1 - THEORETICAL

1. *Lecture*
RYA National Race Training Scheme.
Breakdown of Scheme as a whole — answer questions.

2. *Course prepartation*
- venue (with facilities i.e. boats, lecture room, changing room);
- advertising;
- number of pupils;
- lecture notes in accordance with *G21/82*;
- safety afloat;
- rescue facilities and portable racing marks;
- guest speakers.

3. *RYA Junior Membership*
- advantages;
- cost;
- record cards and badges.

4. *Discussion*
- protest preparations and procedures;
- physical fitness training;
- existing youth training programme and championships;
- Youth Discount Scheme;
- RYA Toppers.

5. *End-of-course discussion*
Pupils' constructive criticism–how to improve the course.

6. *Race Trainer—endorsement/badges.*

DAY 2 - PRACTICAL

1. *Lectures*
Lectures by course candidates on a racing topic (Course Organiser to nominate a twenty minute racing lecture).

2. *Discussion*
Training sessions/exercises afloat.
On completion afloat—practical session covering race training exercises (this will be an assessment).

3. *Debrief, discussion and washup with candidates*
On completion - departure.

Index